VIA

Graduated Readii

VIA PLANA

Graduated Readings in Advanced Latin

P. Ruth Taylor-Briggs

Bristol Classical Press

First published in 2000 by
Bristol Classical Press
an imprint of
Gerald Duckworth & Co. Ltd
61 Frith Street
London W1D 3JL
e-mail: inquiries@duckworth-publishers.co.uk
Website: www.ducknet.co.uk

Reprinted with amendments, 2001

A catalogue record for this book is available from the British Library

ISBN 1-85399-612-2

Printed in Great Britain by
Antony Rowe Ltd., Eastbourne

CONTENTS

***via** tamen opus est incipientibus, sed ea **plana** et cum ad ingrediendum tum ad demonstrandum expedita.*
'However one needs a path for beginners, one which is smooth and uncluttered both for the beginner and for the teacher.'

Quintilian *Inst. Orat.* 8 *praef.*3.

viro carissimo, Andy, et meis tenellulis, Elizabeth atque Jonathan, et ei, quae prima mihi studium litteras Latinas discendi iniecit, Enid Rogers. et praesertim Deo.

Acknowledgements

I would like to express my grateful thanks to those who have helped in the writing of this book: to Desmond Costa and John Betts for their encouragement, careful reading of draft versions and invaluable advice; to David Miller for suggested improvements and changes made in the second edition; to my colleagues at Birmingham for their encouragement; to Kevin Burkhill for his skill, kindness and generosity in supplying the 'road to Rome' on the front cover and to my husband, Andy, for his patient and dedicated proof-reading.

Note to Users

This is the second edition of *VIA PLANA*. Users are alerted to the fact that it contains a number of changes from the first edition; these include amended footnote numbers, especially in Chapter 2.

Bristol Classical Press will be glad of your suggestions for amendments, corrections and improvements which users believe might usefully be incorporated in any future edition. The address for correspondence: Bristol Classical Press, 105 Whiteladies Road, Clifton, Bristol BS8 2PB.

PREFACE

The aims, methods and context of *VIA PLANA*

The main aim of *VIA PLANA* is to guide the modern student along a smooth path to fluency in the reading of *unadapted* Latin authors. Traditionally this skill has been both fostered and tested through the medium of so-called 'unseen translations', a term used to describe random translation exercises provided without a literary or specific pedagogic context. In the days when students routinely learned advanced Latin grammar systematically in so-called 'prose composition' classes (i.e. classes teaching translation from English into Latin), such random unseen translations provided a useful, additional tool for promoting and assessing fluency. However, in the modern educational environment in which prose composition and its concomitant systematic study of advanced Latin grammar are rarely offered, this type of random unseen translation has one major drawback: the students' learning experience arises out of the unrelated and isolated problems encountered in a given extract and thus learning is not only unsystematic but also occurs after, rather than before, the problem/challenge is experienced. *VIA PLANA* aims to counteract this unproductive methodology, going 'back to basics' in teaching principles: following firstly 'Teach the thing before the sign',[1] *VIA PLANA* opens each chapter by presenting in detail a key grammatical construction or related grammatical constructions of the Latin language. Following secondly, 'Teach the easy before the difficult', *VIA PLANA* provides the student with five different levels of exercises/ translation-passages, allowing students even at the lower levels to meet the challenge of unadapted Latin *within* both their skill and their experience level. Following 'Teach one fact at a time...', the translation-passages selected for each chapter of *VIA PLANA* feature prominently the grammar introduced in that chapter, *to the exclusion*, at least in the earlier levels, *of all other grammatical complexities*.

Who is *VIA PLANA* for?

VIA PLANA is suitable both for those approaching advanced Latin grammar for the first time and for those revising, refining and improving their understanding and application of the same. In practice this means that *VIA PLANA* is suitable for A-Level students and post-A-Level undergraduates

---

[1] The principles listed here have been extracted from Mrs Curwen's twelve *Educational Maxims* as expressed in her *Pianoforte Method* of 1886.

(hence the five levels of exercises) and for those who have completed one year of intensive language study as undergraduates or postgraduates etc. It may also be of use to scholarship candidates in the Common Entrance and more ambitious GCSE-students. The structure of *VIA PLANA* is such that teachers of mixed ability classes might find it especially useful (see below, **How to use *VIA PLANA***).

The contents of *VIA PLANA*

VIA PLANA assumes prior knowledge of – and therefore does not cover – basic grammar (i.e. noun-declensions, verb-conjugations etc.). Below the heading of each chapter, however, is a brief section entitled **Parallel Revision**. By following the recommendation in this section to revise a certain aspect of basic grammar (or vocabulary), the student will systematically revise most aspects of Latin grammar in each year of his or her study. Since *VIA PLANA* does not provide grammatical tables, the **Parallel Revision** section refers the student to three so-called 'primers' readily available on the market, i.e. B.H. Kennedy, *The Revised Latin Primer* (London, 1930/1962), or R.M. Griffin, *Cambridge Latin Grammar* (Cambridge, 1991), or James Morwood, *A Latin Grammar* (Oxford, 1999), abbreviated to 'Kennedy', *CLG* and *OLG* respectively. The numbers quoted for the first two are **section** numbers and for *OLG* are **page** numbers.

Each chapter of *VIA PLANA* then proceeds with a description of a grammatical topic.[2] This description again assumes that the student understands the basic terminology of Latin grammar (e.g. words such as 'adjective' or 'participle') but explains all terminology relating to advanced Latin grammar (e.g. 'predicative dative', 'purpose clause' etc.). Once it has been explained, *VIA PLANA* does not shy away from

[2] As indicated above (cf. **The aims, methods and context of *VIA PLANA***), *VIA PLANA* has been written specifically to promote skills required by those translating *from* Latin *into* English, in contrast to the majority of grammar books which, whether consciously or subconsciously, retain the rather obsolete focus on translation from English into Latin. *VIA PLANA*, therefore, relegates such matters as the difference in usage between *iubeo* and *impero* and *quominus* and *quin* to footnotes and likewise does not emphasise the sequence of tenses. Aspects of grammar which are adequately demonstrated by a dictionary (e.g. the difference in usage between *quamquam* and *quamvis*) are also passed over. *VIA PLANA* devotes a full chapter to the relatively basic topic of relative clauses, however, since it is the author's experience that students' understanding of this fundamental aspect of grammar (both in Latin *and* in English) is often little more than instinctive and that this instinctive 'understanding' is liable to fail them in many instances.

using such terminology.[3] Macra are not used to distinguish vowel length in either the illustrations of the text or in the exercises for two reasons: firstly, *VIA PLANA* is intended for students who have already reached a fairly advanced level in their studies and who therefore should be able on their own to recognise and resolve any ambiguities inherent in visually similar/identical forms; secondly, to discourage dependence on a tool which is not normally provided in published texts, the fluent reading of which is the ultimate goal of *VIA PLANA*.

VIA PLANA finally provides various levels of exercises for each chapter. Those chapters featuring a point of grammar considered fairly basic have exercises set only at the lowest two or three levels and those considered most complex do not have exercises set at level one. All other chapters have five levels of exercises, with each level identified by a number, e.g. **Exercise 1**** or **Exercise 3**** etc. The total number of exercises within each level will provide enough course work to cover a full academic year. *VIA PLANA*, therefore, will provide unseen translation material for students over a period of five years. The exercises within each level are of the following type:

Level One (targeted at immediate post-GCSE students or those of equivalent standard, e.g., ambitious GCSE-students, students who have completed one year of intensive study at university or students returning to the study after a break, e.g. those starting university after a 'year out' or mature students)

i) sentences written to test comprehension of the grammar featured; these sentences use *only* the featured grammar, in order to avoid unnecessary distractions from the correct focus;
ii) a similar set of sentences with an extra focus on vocabulary; these 'designated vocabulary exercises' are identified by a superscript 'V', i.e. **Exercise 1B^{V}**; consecutive sentences in these designated vocabulary exercises contain words which are easily confused; extra care should be taken with these words, which are revealed by underlining; for further advice on coping with vocabulary, see below **Coping with vocabulary**.
iii) short extracts of real Latin featuring the relevant grammatical construction(s); instances of the **key grammatical feature** are

[3] For reference purposes, a **Glossary of Technical Terms** has been provided after the **Students' Introduction**.

highlighted in **bold** type, in order to draw the student's attention to them; footnotes provide help, where necessary, but are kept to a minimum by careful extraction of appropriate material; since it cannot be safely assumed that students working at this level have any previous experience of advanced Latin grammar, footnotes in level one contain no cross-referencing to chapters further on in the book but do cross-reference backwards; no cross-referencing is made back to the first chapter on **Relative Clauses**.

Level Two (aimed at students in their A-level year or those of equivalent standard)

i) self-contained sentences extracted from a wide variety of Roman authors; not all chapters include an exercise of this nature, since certain grammatical constructions rely too much on the surrounding context to allow extraction of this sort.

ii) short passages selected from a variety of Roman authors which feature the appropriate grammar; instances of the **key grammatical features** are again highlighted in **bold** type; footnotes provide help, both by cross-referencing to sections in other chapters and also by reference to the **Glossary of Technical Terms**.

Level Three (aimed at first-year undergraduates, more able sixth-formers and those of equivalent standard)

i) passages of moderate length from a wide variety of Latin authors, featuring the **key grammar**; the student's attention is again drawn to instances of this by the use of **bold** type; footnotes continue to provide help but in ever smaller numbers, as no cross-references are made to earlier chapters of the book. Level three, then, withdraws help very gradually and thus encourages students to rely more and more on their own recognition and analysis.

Level Four (aimed at second year undergraduates or students of equivalent standard)

i) passages of Latin of reasonable length with instances of the **key grammatical feature** highlighted in **bold** type; these passages invariably include a variety of other grammatical constructions but no footnotes are provided.

Level Five (aimed at final year undergraduates or students of equivalent standard)

i) longer passages of Latin, featuring the key grammatical feature, usually in the context of a variety of other constructions; no help is provided either by footnotes or by the use of bold type.

How to use *VIA PLANA*

In every year of study, students should, chapter by chapter, study the opening description of the featured grammar and then attempt the exercises/passages at the level appropriate to their ability/experience. Students should not attempt exercises at any higher level until all the chapters of the book have been covered at the level considered appropriate to them individually. They may wish to return to exercises at a lower level, however, for revision purposes. After completing the course at the appropriate level, students should then repeat it at the next level. This structure allows students systematically and comprehensively to encounter or revise a full range of advanced Latin grammar in each year of their study and then in each year to apply their understanding to progressively more difficult tasks. This systematic revision of grammar, each time linked to a more difficult challenge, is the fundamental means by which *VIA PLANA* provides a smooth road to fluency. A useful by-product of this structure, moreover, is that students in mixed-ability classes may easily and conveniently follow the same programme of study but attempt exercises/passages appropriate to their own individual level of ability.

Notes on the selection of individual passages for *VIA PLANA*

The main criteria used in selecting individual passages for *VIA PLANA* were:

i) that they contained enough examples of the relevant grammar to provide sufficient opportunities to test and apply understanding;
ii) in the earlier levels, that they presented no other significant difficulties distracting the focus from the relevant grammar;
iii) that, where the chapter introduced a range of grammatical constructions, the passages corporately, if not individually, also illustrated this range;
iv) that they were of some interest in themselves;
v) that they made sense without their context or with only a small amount of background information;

vi) that they were of an appropriate length to the level for which they are used; a certain amount of flexibility was applied in this respect: some passages considered easier are longer than average for a given level.

As a corpus, the translation-passages selected for *VIA PLANA* may be described as follows:

i) passages selected for levels one to three have been extracted from core authors, largely of the Late Republic and Early Empire, in order to give students a feel for these authors and their works; passages selected for levels four to five, on the other hand, avoid 'core' works or portions of works likely to be used as set texts at undergraduate level (e.g. those currently available in modern editions/commentaries suitable for an undergraduate audience);

ii) over the length of the book, the number of prose and poetry passages is roughly equal; an imbalance of one over the other has been allowed within individual chapters, since certain aspects of grammar occur more in prose than in poetry or *vice versa*;

iii) every effort has been made to ensure that, over the length of the book, the various genres (epic, oratory, history, elegy etc.) are represented in roughly equal measure; certain genres (particularly epic), however, do not offer a ready supply of self-contained passages of a technical nature (i.e. illustrating a number of grammatical constructions) and so are slightly under-represented;

iv) every effort has also been made to ensure that the passages contain 'educational opportunities' beyond those which merely promote fluency. A passage may have strong stylistic features representative of its genre, for example, or may describe something of deep cultural significance to the Roman world (e.g. the ending of the Golden Age), important myths or historical events; it has been left to the initiative of the teacher to make the most of these additional 'educational opportunities'; consecutive passages which have some relationship to each other such that it would be profitable to study them further in conjunction with each other have been labelled **Exercise 1B(i)**, **Exercise 1B(ii)** etc.

v) sources of passages have been given by the name of the author and, where instructive, work only, in order to discourage students from using published translations.

A note on the orthography of passages

Many Latin words allow variant spellings. The Latin for 'path', for example, may be written *uia* or *via*; prefixes are sometimes assimilated, e.g. *afficio*, and sometimes not, e.g. *adficio*; the accusative plural of 'i-stem' third declension nouns is sometimes written *-is* and sometimes *-es* etc. Modern editors of most Latin works reconstruct their texts from manuscripts copied nine centuries or more after their original composition, which do not provide reliable evidence of the author's original spelling. The decisions which they make on orthography, therefore, are largely a question of editorial preference. Since the aim of *VIA PLANA* is to enable the student to cope with reading texts and since these texts represent a diversity of editorial preference, the decision was made to familiarise the student with these differences as part of the process of promoting fluency. Each passage of *VIA PLANA*, therefore, is consistent within itself in orthography but this orthography may vary from passage to passage.

Approaching unseen translations

Fluency in Latin is usually tested by 'unseen translation' exams, in the course of which no help is allowed in the form of tables or dictionaries etc. In order to practise for such exams, students are often encouraged to apply the same restrictions whenever they are required to translate an 'unseen' as part of their coursework. This approach, however, fails to recognize the importance of vocabulary-building in promoting fluency (on which see below, **Students' Introduction**), and ironically through its ban on using a dictionary may stifle progress. A happy compromise can easily be reached by suggesting to the student that he/she first attempts a passage within a given time limit and without any help from dictionaries etc. and then immediately repeats the exercise using a dictionary and any other necessary reference works (e.g. primer, encyclopaedia etc.). Both attempts may be handed in for marking, giving the teacher a clear indication of where the student's strengths and weaknesses lie.

STUDENTS' INTRODUCTION

VIA PLANA provides a context in which you may learn, revise and apply advanced Latin grammar within your own skill level, as explained in the Preface above. The context in which you will learn to apply this understanding of advanced Latin grammar is, at its most elemental level, the vocabulary and phraseology of the Latin language. Learning to cope with vocabulary and phraseology through the use of a dictionary, then, is as much a part of acquiring fluency as learning to understand the grammar. For this reason no vocabulary list has been provided with this book. You should own or have ready access to a dictionary which describes the usage of each word in some detail; it is particularly important that the chosen dictionary should indicate how each word operates within the context of different phrases. *Chambers Murray latin-english Dictionary* (London & Edinburgh, 1933/1976) is excellent in this respect and is still widely available. Too often it is assumed that the use of a dictionary is straightforward and obvious, but the pitfalls into which some students fall over and over again – even those who can quote chapter and verse concerning the grammar – give the lie to this assumption. At the outset, then, you should approach the subject of vocabulary as carefully and methodically as other aspects of the Latin language.

Coping with vocabulary
(i) how to use a Latin-English dictionary

i) Prior to using a good Latin-English dictionary for the first time, make sure that you are familiar with the abbreviations commonly used, e.g. 'Trans.' = 'transitive', 'Transf.' = 'transfigurative (i.e. metaphorical)'; a list of such abbreviations should be found at the front of the dictionary.

ii) Be aware that the meaning listed first in any given entry (particularly of verbs) is often not that most commonly used in the classical period; a good dictionary lists first the original literal meaning, which often became less popular than later transfigurative (i.e. metaphorical) senses evolved from this. Look up, for example, *prodo* and *colo*.

iii) The context in which a word appears is critical to establishing its sense. *fero*, for example, may mean 'I carry', 'I endure', 'I boast', 'I report', 'I publish', 'I propose' etc. You should browse through the various meanings of a word to find the most appropriate for the context. In a good dictionary, this will often become clear by comparison with the lists of the common phrases in which the word appears and/or the short extracts from Latin authors.

iv) Be aware that 'the sum of the parts is often more than the whole'. The meanings appropriate to certain words used individually may, in fact, not be appropriate when they occur within a phrase. The common meanings of *do* and *operam* or *bene* and *facio* used individually, for example, are not appropriate to the same words appearing in the context of the phrases *do operam* or *bene facio*.

v) The form in which a word occurs in its context may be used as a guide in distinguishing between words which are visually similar in their dictionary format: *generibus*, for example, must come from a third (or fourth) declension noun and so is from *genus generis*, meaning 'breeding/race/kind/type', whereas *generos* must come from a second declension noun and so is from *gener generi*, meaning 'son-in-law'; likewise *servavi* must derive from a first conjugation verb, i.e. *servo servare*, meaning 'protect/preserve', whereas *servire* is clearly from a fourth, i.e. *servio servire*, meaning 'be a slave/be obedient'.

Coping with vocabulary
(ii) how to compile a vocabulary book

Not only is it important to take great care in using a dictionary, it is equally important to establish good practice in recording vocabulary both as a learning tool and for speed of re-reading set texts. For this reason it is sensible to create a number of small vocabulary books, one for general use and one for each set text, so that the vocabulary recorded follows the same order as the words are encountered in the text. A vocabulary book may be created as follows:

i) Use a book bound along the long, vertical edge, not at the top. Create a crease down the centre of each page. Put the Latin word to the left of the crease, the English meaning(s) to the right.

ii) For each word, enter as much as is necessary and as little as is possible. Remember that you will later be trying to learn what you have written and that your task will be very daunting if you record every known usage of each word. So, enter the meaning appropriate to the context and, where appropriate, a few of the most common other meanings too.

iii) Good Latin dictionaries record each category of word (e.g. noun, adjective, verb etc.) in a certain format (its 'dictionary format'):

nouns: the nominative singular, genitive singular and gender;

adjectives: the masculine, feminine and neuter nominative singular and any change of stem;

verbs: principal parts in full, except for verbs which conjugate absolutely regularly (i.e. most 1st, 2nd and 4th conjugation verbs).

These formats are themselves a masterpiece of compression. They provide in as succinct a form as possible all that it is necessary for you to know about the form of most words. Without this information, on the other hand, you may encounter difficulty with certain forms. It follows therefore that you should include this 'dictionary format' in your vocabulary book, plus any necessary extra information, e.g. the case which a verb takes (where it is not an accusative).

Coping with vocabulary
(iii) how to learn vocabulary

i) It is essential that you learn the 'dictionary format' of each word, in order to have enough information to analyse all forms, grammatical agreements, etc.

ii) As with physical exercise, 'little and often' is best. You should try to set aside five minutes each day for vocabulary learning rather than half an hour each week.

iii) Good, consistent pronunciation of Latin is invaluable to learning vocabulary. Inconsistent pronunciation does not allow you to 'see' mentally on the page what you are saying, either aloud or in your head, and therefore causes confusion.

GLOSSARY OF TECHNICAL TERMS

The terms listed in this glossary are those used in this book, together with others frequently encountered in other textbooks and commentaries. This glossary does not include the terms of basic Latin grammar, e.g. noun, adjective, etc., knowledge of which is assumed.

accusative of respect	an accusative used to define in what respect an adjective or verb is applicable; the accusative used usually denotes part of the body: *celer pedes*, 'swift in respect of his feet' i.e. 'swift of foot'; *devinctus tempora* 'bound in respect of (your) temples', i.e. '(your) temples bound'.
antecedent	the noun or pronoun to which a relative pronoun refers back (see **1. Relative Clauses A**).
apodosis	the part of a conditional sentence (see **9. Conditional Sentences A**) which expresses the *consequence* of a condition: 'If you continue to do this, *then I will leave*.'
apposition	when a noun is used to describe another noun, the two nouns are said to be 'in apposition' to each other: '*Davus*, *the cook*, prepared a meal.' Nouns 'in apposition' appear in the same case as each other. In this example, they would both be nominative.
clause	a unit of a sentence which contains a subject and a verb; see also **main clause** and **subordinate clause** below.
complement	a word which completes the sense of verbs such as 'I am', 'I become', 'I am called', 'I am considered' etc. It is always in the same case as the subject: 'I (nom.) am *a student/good* etc. (nom.).'
conjunction	a word which links one clause (see above) to another, e.g. 'and', 'but', 'when', 'although' etc.; see also **subordinating conjunction**.
consecutive clause	another name for a result clause (see **6. Purpose and Result Clauses**).

deliberative question	see **8. Independent Subjunctives C**.
final clause	another name for a purpose clause (see **6. Purpose and Result Clauses**).
genitive of characteristic	a genitive found with *est*, in the sense of 'it is', and an infinitive: *est senis meditari.* (lit.) 'it is *of* an old man to contemplate', i.e. 'it is *characteristic of* an old man to contemplate.'
genitive of value	verbs of valuing, considering etc. take a genitive (e.g. *magni, parvi, nihili* etc.) to indicate the extent to which something is valued: *haec nihili habeo.* 'I consider these things *of no value*.'
historic infinitive	an infinitive used in place of a finite verb (one with person endings), where the focus of the description lies more in the action described by the verb than the temporal context within which the action is set; usually a series of historic infinitives occurs in rapid succession but they do sometimes occur singly.
indirect statement/ command/ question	see **2. Indirect Speech**. Some textbooks and commentaries refer to indirect speech as *oratio obliqua* (abbreviated to *o.o.*) and to direct speech as *oratio recta* (abbreviated to *o.r.*).
interrogative pronoun & adjective	these words ask the questions 'Who…?'/'What…?' etc. and 'Which (man/girl/book etc.)' respectively. The interrogative pronoun stands on its own as a question word, whereas the interrogative adjective agrees in case, number and gender with the word it describes, e.g. *quem virum amas?*, 'Which man do you like?'
intransitive verb	a verb which does not take a direct object in the accusative, e.g. verbs of motion, 'I go', 'I come back', or verbs which take a dative or ablative, *parco, utor* etc.
jussive subjunctive	a subjunctive issuing a command or exhortation; see **8. Independent Subjunctives B**.

<table>
<tr><td>main clause</td><td>a clause complete in itself which forms the main element of a sentence and to which i) other clauses may be subordinated (see below subordinate clause) or ii) a second main clause may be added by the use of a conjunction (see above) such as ‘and’ or ‘but’:
i) ‘When you have finished, you may go home.’
ii) ‘I like this one but you like that one.’</td></tr>
<tr><td>mood</td><td>i.e. indicative, imperative or subjunctive, for which see 8. Independent Subjunctives A.</td></tr>
<tr><td>predicate</td><td>the part of the sentence which describes the subject (see 3. Predicative Datives A).</td></tr>
<tr><td>protasis</td><td>the part of a conditional sentence which expresses the condition: ‘If you continue to do this, then I will leave.’; see 9. Conditional Sentences A.</td></tr>
<tr><td>reflexive</td><td>a word used to describe the pronoun se and the adjective, suus –a –um, which (usually) refer back to the third person subject of the main verb.</td></tr>
<tr><td>sequence of tenses</td><td>the tense of a subjunctive in most subordinate clauses is governed by the tense of the verb in the main clause:
<table>
<tr><th>Tense of main verb</th><th>Tense of subjunctive</th></tr>
<tr><td>Present
Future
Perfect ‘I have loved’
Imperative</td><td>Present
(occasionally Perfect)</td></tr>
<tr><td>Imperfect
Perfect ‘I loved’
Pluperfect</td><td>Imperfect
or
Pluperfect</td></tr>
</table>
Normally the sequence of tenses is of little significance to those translating from Latin into English. However, when the verb used in the main clause has third person singular forms which are visually identical in the present and perfect tenses</td></tr>
</table>

	(e.g. *accidit*), the tense of subjunctive found in the subordinate clause clarifies the tense of indicative used in the main clause: *venit ut Britanniam vincat.* (*present* subj., so *pres.* indicative) 'He is coming in order to conquer Britain.' *venit ut Britanniam vinceret.* (*imperfect* subj., so *perfect* indicative) 'He came in order to conquer Britain.'
subordinate clause	a **clause** incomplete in itself, both grammatically and in sense, which provides more information about the action or situation described in the **main clause**. So, the temporal clause '*When he realised what trouble he was in*, and the purpose clause '*in order to conceal the truth*' are incomplete in themselves but indicate both the time at which and the purpose for which 'he lied': '*When he realised what trouble he was in*, he lied *in order to conceal the truth*.'
subordinating conjunction	a **conjunction** which introduces a **subordinate clause**, e.g. 'since', 'in order to' etc.
supine	the form of the supine is that of the perfect participle ending either in *–um* or in *–u*, e.g. *dictum*, *dictu*. The supine ending in *–um* is found after verbs of motion and indicates purpose: *venit Britanniam victum* 'He came (in order to) conquer Britain.' The supine ending in *–u* is found after certain adjectives and a very small number of nouns (e.g. *fas, nefas*); translate 'to…': *hoc est facile factu.* 'This is easy *to do*.'
transitive verb	a verb which takes a direct object in the accusative.
voice	i.e. active or passive. An active verb is one where the subject carries out the action of the verb: 'The cat *caught* the mouse.' A passive verb is one where the subject has the action of the verb done to it: 'The mouse *was caught* by the cat.'

Chapter 1

RELATIVE CLAUSES

Parallel Revision: Forms of the Relative Pronoun, Kennedy 97, CLG 5.7, OLG pp. 27-8.

A. What is a Relative Clause?

A relative clause is a clause introduced by a relative pronoun, in English the words 'who', 'which', 'whom' or 'whose'. In function, it is an adjectival clause since it *describes* a noun or pronoun. In the sentence,

> 'The boy, who was sitting in the amphitheatre, admired the gladiators' skill.'

for example, the clause 'who was sitting in the amphitheatre' describes 'The boy'. The noun (or pronoun) described by a relative clause has a special name, the **antecedent**. In the above sentence, therefore, 'The boy' is the antecedent.

B. How do Relative Clauses work?

The advantage of a relative clause is that it enables two simple sentences to be combined into one by subordinating the one to the other. The single sentence given above, for example, may be said to subordinate the simple sentence 'The boy was sitting in the amphitheatre' to a second simple sentence 'The boy admired the gladiators' skill'. This subordination is achieved by taking the *repeated* noun ('The boy') from the first sentence and by replacing it with the relative pronoun, here 'who'. This relative pronoun *represents* the noun (or pronoun) which it has replaced, which was, of course, the same noun as the antecedent.

i) The gender and number of the relative pronoun.

Since the relative pronoun *represents* a noun which is the same as the antecedent, logically the **gender and number** of the relative pronoun are the **same as** the gender and number of **the antecedent.**[1]

ii) The case of the relative pronoun.

The **case** of the relative pronoun is determined by its **function within its own clause**. So if the relative pronoun is the subject of its own clause, it will occur in the nominative case; if it is the object of its own clause, it will occur in the accusative, etc. In order to establish most simply in one's own mind what function the relative pronoun has in its own clause, replace it with the original noun or pronoun and convert the clause into an independent sentence. For example, from

'The book, which I bought yesterday, is interesting.'

revert to two separate sentences:

'I bought *a book* yesterday. The book is interesting.'

This backwards process clearly reveals that 'a book', the noun represented by the relative pronoun 'which' in the relative clause, is the object of the verb 'I bought'. Therefore, as much as it must be accusative in this separate sentence, so it will be accusative when replaced by the relative pronoun in the relative clause.

In summary, the relative pronoun:

- takes its number and gender from its antecedent
- takes its case from its function within its own clause.

C. How do we translate a relative pronoun?

There are two issues involved in translating a relative pronoun. Firstly, one must establish which word is its antecedent. Secondly, it is necessary to decide which English form of the pronoun it is appropriate to use.

---

[1] For a few exceptions to this rule, see Kennedy 332.

i) Identifying the antecedent of the relative pronoun.

The relative pronoun has the same gender and number as its antecedent. Therefore, in order to identify its antecedent, identify first the gender and number of the relative pronoun (bear in mind that there may be more than one possibility) and then look for another word of the same gender and number in the same sentence. An antecedent usually, but not always, precedes the relative clause. If there are two or more nouns of the same gender and number as the relative pronoun in the remainder of the sentence, the antecedent will usually be the one closest in position to the relative pronoun.
NB: the case of the relative pronoun is completely irrelevant when attempting to identify its antecedent!
Occasionally, when reference is being made to some general category of people or things, the antecedent is omitted. The English language does not like this omission and so an appropriately general antecedent must be supplied by observing the context carefully. For example,

> *sunt qui mores alienos semper suspicantur.*

allows the translation

> 'There are *men* who are always suspicious of other people's characters.'

since the relative pronoun is masculine and plural.

ii) Deciding which English form of the relative pronoun to use.

As in Latin, the relative pronoun in English has more than one form, 'who', 'whom', 'whose' and 'which'. English uses 'who', 'whom' and 'whose' to refer to people and 'which' to refer to animals and things. When a relative pronoun refers to people, we choose between 'who', 'whom' and 'whose' according to its function within its clause. These functions generally correlate to the cases used in Latin. So where Latin uses a nominative form of the relative pronoun, the appropriate form in English is usually the word 'who'; where Latin uses an accusative form, the appropriate English form is usually 'whom'.[2] Generally speaking, therefore, it is possible to say that for a given case in Latin a given form of the relative pronoun in English is appropriate in accordance with the following table:

Case in Latin	**English:** when the antecedent is a **person**	**English**: when the antecedent is a **thing**
Nominative	'who'	'which'
Accusative	'whom'	'which'
Genitive	'whose', 'of whom'	'of which', 'whose'
Dative	'to/for whom' etc.; or 'whom' with verbs which take the dative	'to/for which' etc.; or 'which' with verbs which take the dative
Ablative	'by/with whom' etc.; or 'whom' with verbs which take the ablative	'by/with which' etc.; or 'which' with verbs which take the ablative

Students working at Level One should now attempt the Preliminary Exercise and Exercise 1A on pp. 7-8

D. The Relative Adjective

The forms of the relative pronoun can also function as adjectives, in which case they describe a noun with which they agree in case, number and gender. A relative adjective is usually found in two circumstances:

i) where the antecedent is repeated in the relative clause:

---

[2] Although little used in modern English, it is a useful discipline to use 'whom' as an initial translation of the accusative of the relative pronoun as a means of establishing in one's mind the precise function of the Latin form.

complures praeterea minores subiectae insulae existimantur, de quibus insulis non nulli scripserunt... (Caesar)

'Several smaller *islands* besides are thought to lie near, concerning which islands some have written...

ii) where the noun with which the relative adjective agrees is a synonym for or a general description of the word or phrase which is logically, but not grammatically, the antecedent:

ex eis omnibus longe sunt humanissimi qui Cantium incolunt, quae regio est maritima omnis... (Caesar)

'Of all of these by far the most humane are those who inhabit *Kent*, *which region* is entirely maritime... '

As the above two examples reveal, the most appropriate translation of a relative adjective is by the word '**which**'.

E. The 'Connecting' Relative

i) What is a 'connecting' relative?

Latin frequently opens a sentence with a relative pronoun, even where, in order to do so, this pronoun must displace another word (e.g. a conjunction such as *ubi*, *cum* etc.) from its normal position first in a clause. Where this happens, the antecedent will normally be found (by applying the normal rules) in the preceding sentence.[3] A relative pronoun of this type is called a 'connecting' relative since it highlights the connection between one sentence and the next. The 'connecting' relative achieves this by showing that the same

[3] An antecedent may not be found where a neuter pronoun is used as the connecting relative; see below, section **E** iii). A relative pronoun *may* also appear first in a sentence if the relative clause precedes the clause by which it is governed, in which case the antecedent will be expressed later in the sentence (the antecedent will still be identified by following the rules indicated in section **C** i) above). Instances of a relative clause preceding the clause by which it is governed, however, are comparatively rare.

subject matter (i.e. that of the antecedent) is carried over from the previous sentence.

ii) **How do we translate a 'connecting' relative?**

The English language neither uses a relative pronoun to open a sentence nor allows a pronoun to disrupt normal word order. In place of a 'connecting' relative, therefore, English uses either '**him**', '**her**', '**it**', '**them**' etc., or some form of the pronoun '**this**' and puts it in an appropriate position within the clause:

> *nuntius multas res gravissimas consuli detulit. quas ubi audivit, consul senatum convocavit.*
>
> 'The messenger reported many very serious matters to the consul. When he had heard *them*, the consul called a meeting of the senate.'

iii) **The use of a neuter pronoun as a 'connecting' relative.**

When a 'connecting' relative occurs in the neuter singular or plural, it does not always have a specific antecedent in the previous sentence but sometimes picks up the general idea or ideas encapsulated in this previous sentence:

> *testis palluit, verba incohata interrupit, oculos deiectos avertit. quae ubi iudices conspexerunt, testimonium pro falso habebant.*
>
> 'The witness grew pale, broke off the words he had begun, turned aside his downcast eyes. When the judges observed *these things*, they considered his evidence false.'

Exercises for Level One

Preliminary Exercise

The aim of this exercise is to reinforce understanding of the basic principles of relative clauses by concentrating in English on the relative pronoun. For each sentence, first identify the relative pronoun and then the antecedent. Establish what gender and number the antecedent must be and therefore what gender and number the relative pronoun must be. Then consider carefully what case the relative pronoun should be in and give its appropriate form in Latin. Finally it will be instructive to observe what case the antecedent would be in.

a) Clodia, who used to love Catullus, now loves someone else.
b) I will find something with which I can break down this door.
c) I quite like that man whom you hate.
d) Did you give food to the old woman to whom you also gave money?
e) The girl, whose mother died recently, is distraught with grief.
f) The father of the girl, whose beauty is second to none, has given her a huge dowry.
g) The book (*m.*), which you decided not to read, is actually very interesting.
h) Who is the man to whom you were speaking just now?
i) This book is longer than that one which you are now enjoying.[4]
j) I praised Marcus, who had studied very hard.

---

[4] Bear in mind that the Latin for 'enjoy' is *fruor*.

Exercise 1A

a) hominem valde timeo qui suam uxorem trucidavit.
b) sorores, quarum mater aberat, laetae ludebant.
c) pueri diligenter magistro operam dabant, qui litteras Latinas docebat.
d) feminamne scis quam omnes pulcherrimam habent?
e) omnes puellae pueros quibus di magnas divitias dederunt semper amant.
f) rationem scio qua optimi coqui optimam cenam coquunt.
g) ille, qui multum auctoritatis apud iudices habet, testes periurare iussit.
h) homines quibus Caesar parcit semper ei maximas gratias agunt.
i) illi ego qui parentes egentes reliquit deseruitque honorem reddere non possum.
j) ea quae supervacanea sunt eximere oportet.

Exercise 1B[V]

a) omnibus Britannis, quae gentes bellicosissimae sunt, sunt multi <u>mores</u> inusitati.
b) biduum milites insidiabantur, qua <u>mora</u> rationes hostium melius cognoscere poterant.
c) <u>hostium</u> aditus nostri vallo fossaque interclusere. quo facto praesidia paribus intervallis disposuere.
d) <u>hostiarum</u> exta haruspices aestate ineunte interpretabantur, quo tempore Sulla bellum renovare parabat.
e) Midas omnia a se tacta in aurum verti voluit. quod ubi ei datum est, nihil omnino <u>esse</u> poterat pauperiorque re vera fiebat.
f) ad laevam <u>est</u> fanum Cereris. quod ubi ingressus eris, statuam miro artificio e marmore fictam invenies.
g) saltare aliquos iuvat, quae delectatio tamen apud Romanos pro indignissimo habetur.

Exercise 1C

Caesar describes the basic geography of Britain.

insula natura triquetra, **cuius** unum latus est contra Galliam. huius lateris alter angulus, **qui** est ad Cantium, quo[5] fere omnes ex Gallia naves appelluntur, ad orientem solem[6], inferior[7] ad meridiem spectat. hoc pertinet circiter milia passuum quingenta. alterum[8] vergit ad Hispaniam atque occidentem solem; **qua** ex parte est Hibernia, dimidio minor, ut existimatur, quam Britannia, sed pari spatio transmissus atque ex Gallia est in Britanniam[9]. in hoc medio cursu est insula **quae** appellatur Mona... huius est longitudo lateris, ut fert illorum opinio, septingentorum milium. tertium[10] est contra septentriones, **cui** parti nulla est obiecta terra; sed eius angulus lateris maxime ad Germaniam spectat. hoc milia passuum octingenta in longitudinem esse existimatur. ita omnis insula est in circuitu vicies centum milium passuum.

Caesar, *Bellum Gallicum*

---

[5] *quo*: '(to) where…'.
[6] *ad orientem solem*: supply *spectat* from the end of the sentence.
[7] *inferior*: understand *angulus*.
[8] *alterum*: understand *latus*.
[9] *pari spatio...Britanniam*: 'set apart from Britain by an equal distance as from Gaul.'
[10] *tertium*: understand *latus*.

Exercises for Level Two

Exercise 2A

a) ira quae tegitur nocet. (Seneca)

b) sed nihil, quod crudele, utile. (Cicero)

c) tune es ille, quo senatus carere non potuit? (Cicero)

d) ante mare et terras et quod tegit omnia caelum
unus erat toto naturae vultus in orbe,
quem dixere chaos. (Ovid)

e) saepe aliquis digito vatem designat euntem,
atque ait 'hic, hic est, quem ferus urit Amor!' (Ovid)

f) 'o fortunati, quorum iam moenia surgunt!' (Virgil)

g) tum pater Anchises: 'animae, quibus altera fato
corpora debentur, Lethaei ad fluminis undam
securos latices et longa oblivia potant. (Virgil)

h) qui videt, is peccat: qui te non viderit ergo,
non cupiet: facti lumina crimen habent. (Propertius)

Exercise 2B

Ovid begs Augustus for a reduction in his punishment.

parce, uir inmenso maior uirtutibus orbe,
iustaque uindictae supprime lora tuae.
parce, precor, saecli decus indelebile nostri,
terrarum dominum **quem** sua cura facit.
per patriae nomen, **quae** te tibi carior ipso est,
per numquam surdos in tua uota deos,
perque tori sociam, **quae** par tibi sola reperta est,
et **cui** maiestas non onerosa tua est,
perque tibi similem uirtutis imagine natum,
moribus adgnosci **qui** tuus esse potest,
perque tuos uel auo dignos uel patre nepotes,
qui ueniunt magno per tua iussa gradu,
parte leua minima nostras et contrahe poenas,
daque, procul Scythico **qui** sit[11] ab hoste, locum.

Ovid, *Epistulae ex Ponto*

[11] For the subjunctive, see **6. Purpose and Result Clauses Part 2 B**.

Chapter 2
INDIRECT SPEECH

> Parallel Revision: Forms of Infinitives, Kennedy 115-25, CLG 7f.6-11, OLG pp. 37-60.

Part 1. What is indirect speech?

Verbs which express or imply speech or thought, e.g. verbs of saying, asserting, thinking, asking, wondering, complaining, hearing etc., sometimes take a simple direct object, expressed in Latin by the accusative case: e.g.,

English	Latin
'He declared his innocence.'	*innocentiam affirmabat.*
'She begged his forgiveness.'	*veniam ab eo petiit.*
'They asked a question (lit. something).'	*aliquid rogabant.*

The objects in these simple sentences, the words 'innocence', 'forgiveness' and 'question' respectively, are interchangeable with longer clauses beginning, e.g., with 'that...' or with 'to...' or with question words:

'He declared *that he had never done anything wrong.*'

'She begged him *to forgive her.*'

'They asked *who would be in charge of the army.*'

Since these clauses are interchangeable with a simple direct object, they are called object-clauses.[1] Although these object-clauses give more information about what was originally said

---

[1] The *subject* of some sentences may also be replaced by clauses of this nature. So, the subject of 'The defendant's guilt is obvious.' can be replaced by a 'that'-clause:

'*That the defendant is guilty* is obvious.'

Since it is the subject that is replaced by the clause in these cases, these clauses are called 'subject-clauses'. They are less common than the object-clauses described above, but the same rules apply to their construction in Latin.

than the simple direct objects, they still do not express the precise words of the speaker in their original format. The precise words of the speaker might in fact have been, respectively:

'I have never done anything wrong.'

'Forgive me!'

'Who will be in charge of the army?'

Each of these last three sentences is an example of direct speech, quoting exactly the speaker's own words. The object-clauses in the previous set of sentences, on the other hand, are examples of *indirect* speech for the very reason that they do *not* express the speaker's precise words in their original format.

Direct speech is sub-divided into three main categories,[2] i.e. statements, commands and questions. In the same way, indirect speech shows the same three sub-divisions. Latin has its own ways of expressing each of these sub-divisions of indirect speech.[3]

---

[2] For a fourth sub-division, see **8. Independent Subjunctives D**.

[3] It is the type of speech governed by the introductory verb and not the introductory verb itself that determines whether a clause is an indirect statement, question or command. Some introductory verbs may govern more than one type of indirect speech. Consider the following pairs of sentences:

1a) I know that you are tired.

1b) I know how to do this.

2a) I heard that you were coming for the festival.

2b) I heard which subjects you decided to study.

In each pair, the sentence marked a) does contain an indirect statement, reporting the direct *statement*, respectively:

'You are tired.'

'You are coming for the festival.'

The same verbs in both b) examples, on the other hand, introduce *indirect questions*, reporting the original *questions*, respectively:

'How do I do this?'

'Which subjects did you decide to study?'

Part 2. Indirect Statements

(i) The Basics

In English, indirect statements are statements introduced by the word 'that...'[4] as the object of a verb (or sometimes a noun) expressing or implying speech or thought; the remainder of the indirect statement is constructed normally: e.g.

I hear *that you succeeded.*

I know *that the earth is round.*

They realised *that their friend had told a lie.*

The commander received a message *that the enemy had laid an ambush.*

In Latin, there is no equivalent at all to the introductory word 'that...'. Instead, Latin uses a part of the verb and a case of the noun different from those which express the subject and verb in *direct* statements to show the existence of an *indirect* statement. Indirect statements in Latin are in fact often descriptively labelled 'accusative and infinitive constructions' since the subject of an indirect statement is always in the **accusative** case and the verb always in the **infinitive**. So:

A. The **subject** of an indirect statement:

i) is *always* in the **accusative** case;

ii) is almost *always expressed.* This means that, whereas in direct speech the subject is often *in* the verb (i.e. *aquam portat* means '*s/he* carries the water', without the use of a pronoun to express 's/he'), in indirect speech it is usually expressed at the very least by a pronoun such as *is*, *ea*, *id*:[5]

---

[4] Sometimes 'that…' is omitted, as in 'I know the earth is round.'

[5] Exceptions to this rule occur where the verb of an indirect statement is impersonal (e.g. *placet* 'it pleases', *licet* 'it is allowed', *oportet* 'it is right' etc.) or where the verb 'to be' is used in the sense of 'there is/are'.

audivi eos matrem necavisse.

'I heard that they had killed their mother.'

iii) is represented, when expressing the third person (i.e. 'he', 'she', 'they' etc.), by the reflexive pronoun *se,* if it is the *same* as the subject of the introductory verb; on the other hand, if the subjects of the introductory verb and indirect statement are *different*, then other pronouns are used, e.g., *eum/eam/id* etc. So,

dixit se aegrotavisse.

'He said that he (i.e. *himself*) had been unwell.'

is clearly differentiated from

dixit eum aegrotavisse.

'He said that he (i.e. *someone else*) had been unwell.'

Similarly, the reflexive adjective *suus -a -um* is usually used where by 'his/her' or 'their' the intention is to refer back to the subject of the main introductory verb of the sentence. So,

Marcus Gaio dixit suam amicam infidelem esse.

means

'Marcus told Gaius that his (i.e. his own) girlfriend was unfaithful.'

whereas

Marcus Gaio dixit eius amicam infidelem esse.

means

'Marcus told Gaius that his (i.e. Gaius') girlfriend was unfaithful.'

B. The **verb** of an indirect statement:

i) is always in the **infinitive**;

ii) shows in the tense of this infinitive the tense of finite verb that would have been used in the original *direct* utterance. So, the direct statement

Romam adiit

'He went to Rome.'

using a perfect indicative, when reported in an indirect statement uses a perfect infinitive:

Cicero mihi dixit se Romam adiisse.

'Cicero told me that he had gone to Rome.'

iii) is sometimes abbreviated by the omission of *esse*. This applies to those infinitives which are created by adding *esse* to perfect or future participles, i.e. future active and deponent infinitives and perfect deponent and passive infinitives. So, *missos* appears in place of *missos esse* or *capturum* in place of *capturum esse*:

victores sperabant se magnam praedam adepturos.

'The victorious [soldiers] hoped that they would gain much booty.'

Part 3. Indirect Statements
(ii) Five Tips for Translation

i) Although out of context the pronoun *se* can be either singular or plural and of any gender and although, correspondingly, the reflexive adjective *suus -a -um* may mean either 'his', 'her' or 'their' etc., since both words normally refer back to the subject of the *main* verb, it is the identity of this subject that indicates how each instance should be translated. So, in the sentence

puella putat se pulcherrimam esse.

since the subject of the main verb is female and singular, *se* must mean 'she':

'The girl thinks that *she* is very beautiful.'

In the example given above (p.15),

Marcus Gaio dixit suam amicam infidelem esse.

since the subject of the main verb is *Marcus*, both masculine and singular, *suam* should be translated 'his (own)'.

ii) If the introductory verb is present or future or an imperative, translate the tense of the infinitive in the indirect statement ordinarily: so,

Introductory Verb	Tense of Infinitive	Translation of Infinitive
'He says/will say/Say!...	**present**	'that x is happening.'
'He says/will say/Say!...	**future**	'that x will happen.'
'He says/will say/Say!...	**perfect**	'that x (has) happened.'

When the introductory verb is in a past tense, however, English has its own idiomatic ways of expressing tenses in indirect statements. So, after an introductory verb in a past tense, translate:

Introductory Verb	Tense of Infinitive	Translation of Infinitive
'He said/had said...	**present**	'that x was happening.'
'He said/had said...	**future**	'that x would happen.'
'He said/had said...	**perfect**	'that x had happened.'

So:

dixit se assidue studere. (**present** infinitive)
'He said that he *was studying* hard.'
affirmabant se equos venditūros esse. (**future** infinitive)
'They indicated that they *would sell* the horses.'
confirmavi me puellam punivisse. (**perfect** infinitive)
'I confirmed that I *had punished* the girl.'

iii) In Latin, where *nego* introduces an indirect statement, it usually expresses 'I *say* that x does *not* happen' (<u>not</u> 'I do not say that'). Similarly, *nego...quemquam/umquam/usquam* etc. should be translated 'I say that no-one/...never.../... nowhere...' etc. rather than 'I do not say that anyone/...ever...' etc. English idiom in fact requires us to take the negative contained in *nego* out of the introductory verb and put it into the indirect statement.

iv) Although in Latin there is no word corresponding to the English word 'that', this word should *always* be added to your translation, immediately after the introductory verb or phrase and before the indirect statement. When you first practise translating simple indirect statements, you may be tempted to imagine that this word is not important. After all,

'I thought him to be sensible.'

is acceptable English and means exactly the same as

'I thought that he was sensible'.

This construction without 'that', however, works only for the most simple indirect statements in English, whereas in Latin indirect statements can be fairly lengthy. Therefore, it is a good idea right at the outset to get into the habit of adding the word 'that' to your translation as soon as you notice the existence of an indirect statement by observing the presence of an accusative and infinitive construction.

v) In Latin, where a number of indirect statements follow on from each other, the introductory verb is usually not repeated. This happens because the continued use of the accusative and infinitive construction shows very economically that these statements are still indirect. The English language, on the other hand, cannot be so economical in indicating the continuation of indirect speech. Consequently, when you have found a series of accusative and infinitive constructions in a Latin passage and have concluded that they express a string of indirect statements, in your English translation it is usually sensible to add extra appropriate introductory verbs at reasonable intervals, e.g. 'He went on to say that...' or 'He added that...' or 'He continued by saying that...' etc.

Students working at Level One should now attempt Exercises 1A and 1B on pp. 26.

Part 4. Indirect Statements
(iii) Further Facts

C. Second indirect statements dependent on the first. An indirect statement can itself govern a second indirect statement. Consider:

'He said that he had heard that Rome was burning.'

Here, the main verb of the sentence, 'He said...', introduces the indirect statement 'that he had heard...'. This indirect statement in turn introduces a further indirect statement, 'that Rome was burning.' The same rules apply to this second indirect statement as applied to the first. Hence, the Latin for this sentence would be:

dixit se audivisse Romam ardescere.

D. Avoidance of the future infinitive. Latin often avoids the use of future infinitives (particularly future passive infinitives) in indirect statements by replacing the normal accusative and infinitive construction with either *futurum esse ut* or *fore ut* + subjunctive, i.e. with the future infinitive of the verb 'to be' (in either of its two forms) followed by *ut* + subjunctive. In this context, *futurum esse/fore ut* + subjunctive literally means 'that it will be the case that...'. When encountering this formula, you may initially wish to translate literally to gain an understanding of the intended sense, then rephrase to produce more fluent English. For example, *spero fore ut hoc officium tibi prosit.*

translated literally as

'I hope that it will be that this task is of use to you.'

becomes

'I hope that this task will be of use to you.'

After a little practice, it should be possible to by-pass this first stage of literal translation.

E. The subjunctive in subordinate clauses within indirect speech. Subordinate clauses within indirect speech usually take a subjunctive verb. This is to show that these clauses belong to the words of the speech being reported and are not an insertion by the author or narrator for the sake of providing some information or explanation.[6] For example, the relative clause in the sentence

The consul stated that those *who had committed a crime* would be punished.

is part of the statement being reported, namely,

'Those *who have committed a crime* will be punished.'

and as such will contain a subjunctive verb when it occurs in the context of the indirect speech:

consul declarabat fore ut ii, qui crimen commisissent, punirentur.

Since the subjunctive is used in this subordinate clause merely as a means of indicating to whom the words belong, it is not necessary to add any extra 'special' sense, such as 'should' or 'would' in translation.

---

[6] Since it is normal practice to use the subjunctive in subordinate clauses within indirect speech to show that the clauses belong to the speech being reported, on the few occasions where the author or narrator wants to insert his own additional, explanatory information into indirect speech, he can show this very economically by using the indicative in place of the subjunctive. So, the clause *quorum ei copia in urbe contigerat*, for example, in line 4 of **Exercise 1D** later in this chapter, shows by the use of the indicative that this is an extra piece of information that the author (Tacitus) is adding to provide the reader with information beyond that which belongs to the reported speech.

Students working at Level One should now attempt Exercises 1C and 1D on p. 27.

Part 5. Indirect Commands

Indirect commands are commands reported not in their original format, but as the object of introductory verbs (or occasionally nouns) of commanding, urging, persuading, encouraging, begging[7] etc. In English, indirect commands are constructed in two ways,

i) '(not) to...'
ii) 'that x should (not)...'

as illustrated by the italicised portions of the following sentences:

'They persuaded her *to give herself up.*'
'I suggested *that they should consult the oracle.*'
'She begged me *not to do it.*'

The 'command'-nature of each of these italicised clauses becomes readily apparent after conversion back into direct speech:

'Give yourself up!'
'Consult the oracle!'
'Please don't do it!'

each of which sentences requires the use of an imperative or equivalent construction for its translation into Latin:

te dede!
oraculum consulite!
noli hoc facere!

---

[7] Surprisingly excluded from the normal construction of indirect commands in Latin are two common verbs, *iubere* 'to order' and *vetare* 'to forbid'. In parallel with the most common English construction, both verbs take the accusative of the person who is ordered to do something and the infinitive of the thing that they are ordered to do; e.g., *te hoc facere iubet* means 'He orders you (acc.) to do (inf.) this' and *eos venire vetuimus* means 'We forbade them (acc.) to come (inf.).'

A. The construction of indirect commands. After the verb (or noun) introducing the indirect command, Latin uses:

- i) *ut*[8] + subjunctive to express a positive command;
- ii) *ne* + subjunctive to express a negative command;
- iii) *neu* or *neve* + subjunctive to add a second negative command to the first.

The three sample sentences given above can therefore be translated respectively:

ei persuadebant ut ipsam dederet.
eos monebam ut oraculum consulerent.
me orabat ne illud facerem.

B. Se/suus etc. As with indirect statements, where the reflexive pronoun and adjective *se/suus* occur in indirect commands, they normally refer back to the 3rd person subject of the main verb.

C. Extended indirect speeches. Just as indirect speeches may consist of a series of indirect statements (see above, pp. 18-19), so they may also contain a mixture of different elements, i.e. indirect statements, commands and questions. Where an indirect command occurs as the second or a subsequent element of such an extended speech, *ut* is often omitted from its opening. The clause should however remain readily identifiable as an indirect command, since it is common editorial practice to separate the individual elements of an extended reported speech by using semi-colons (;). Semi-colons occurring after indirect speech has begun, then, suggest that the indirect speech continues and that a clause containing only a subjunctive verb is an indirect command:

---

[8] *uti* is sometimes found in place of *ut*.

Laocoon Troianos monebat ut equum ligneum extra moenia linquerent; Danaos etiam dona ferentes timerent; eum in pelagus praecipitarent.

'Laocoon warned the Trojans that they should leave the wooden horse outside the walls; that they should fear the Greeks even when they were bearing gifts; that they should hurl the horse into the sea.'

ne is not omitted in this situation since it is needed to provide the negative for the clause.

Students working at Level One should now attempt Exercises 1E and 1F on pp. 28.

Part 6. Indirect Questions

These are questions reported not in the speaker's original words but as object-clauses after verbs (and occasionally nouns) of asking, knowing, telling, wondering etc., as shown by the italicised portions of the following sentences:

'He wondered *whether he would ever see her again*.'

'He asked *when he would be able to go*.'

The 'question'-nature of these clauses of indirect speech is evident after conversion back into direct speech, i.e. the speaker's original words, where the above indirect questions will respectively become the direct questions:

'Will I ever see her again?'

'When will I be able to go?'

A. The basics

Indirect questions in Latin open with a **question word** and then have their verb in the **subjunctive**.

B. Common question words

Question word	Translation
quis, quid etc.	'who', 'what' etc.
quid	'why'
quantus	'how great', 'what a great…'
qualis	'what sort of'
cur, quamobrem, qua ex re, quare	'why'
ubi	'where' but NOT 'when'
quando, quo tempore	'when'
ut	'how'
num, -ne[9]	'whether'
utrum…an, -ne…an	'whether…or'
utrum…necne, -ne…necne	'whether…or not'

C. Indirect questions referring to the future

Since Latin does not have a future subjunctive, indirect questions referring to the future are sometimes expressed by using a future participle (e.g. *mansurus)* with either the present or the imperfect subjunctive of the verb 'to be', respectively *sim, sis, sit* or *essem, esses, esset* etc., as appropriate:[10]

> *Naso nesciebat utrum ab exsilio regressurus esset necne.*
>
> 'Ovid did not know whether he would ever return from exile or not.'

---

[9] *-ne* is attached to the word around which the question revolves and is positioned first in the question.

[10] The use of the present or the imperfect subjunctive depends on the sequence of tenses, for which see the **Glossary of Technical Terms**.

D. Se/suus etc. As in indirect statements and commands, the reflexive pronoun and adjective *se/suus* are normally used to refer back to the 3rd person subject of the main verb.[11]

Students working at Level One should now attempt Exercises 1G^V, 1H & 1J on pp. 29-30.

[11] See above, **2. Indirect Speech Part 2 A** iii).

Exercises for Level One

Exercise 1A: Indirect Statements (i)

This exercise allows you to see whether you have understood the basic principles of indirect statements. It consists of five pairs of sentences which differ from each other only in detail. Look carefully at these differences in detail and, using the grammatical explanations provided above, work out for yourself what effect they make.

1a) dicit se puellam vidisse.
1b) dicit eum puellam vidisse.
2a) sperant se hostes victuros esse.
2b) uxores sperant eos hostes victuros esse.
3a) nuntius affirmat Gallos captos esse.
3b) nuntius affirmavit Gallos captos esse.
4a) dominus promittit se magnum praemium servo fideli daturum esse.
4b) dominus promittebat se magnum praemium servo fideli daturum esse.
5a) Cicero negat se omnium poetarum optimum esse.
5b) Cicero negabat se omnium poetarum optimum esse.

Exercise 1B: Indirect Statements (ii)

a) Cicero negavit se ullas litteras a Quinto fratre accepisse.
b) imperator nuntium accepit classem hieme perditam esse.
c) Daedalum omnium inventorem artium fuisse ferunt.
d) omnes rumorem audierant regem iam decessisse.
e) rhetores docent oratorem minime irasci decere.
f) iudices suspicabantur reum mentiri.
g) captivi tandem confitebantur se patriam prodidisse.
h) constat navigationem hieme periculosissimam esse.
i) Plinius scripsit se iam mentem ad philosophiam appellere.
j) placet bellum omnibus Gallis inferre necesse esse.

Exercise 1C: Indirect Statements (iii)

a) credo fore ut Romani Poenos vincant.
b) audio Marcum, cuius mater mortua sit, dolore confici.
c) fama est praetores negasse se ulla spectacula praebituros.
d) aliqui dicunt futurum ut totus mundus mox deleatur.
e) rumorem audivi barbaros credere nullos deos esse.
f) speculatores imperatori dixere hostes, quandocumque frumentarentur, castra incustodita relinquere.
g) puer patri pollicebatur fore ut se coram maioribus natu optime gereret.
h) mater maesta suspicabatur fore ut filius unicus numquam a bello reverteretur.
i) Ariadne identidem querebatur Thesea pollicitum esse se fidelem futurum esse.
j) ille explicabat servos, quos magno emisset, artifices esse.

Exercise 1D: Indirect Statements (iv)

Cicero's education.

[You know Cicero's book, 'Brutus', in which he relates, as it were, the 'nurturing' of his eloquence]: **se** apud Q. Mucium ius civile **didicisse**, apud Philonem Academicum, apud Diodotum Stoicum omnes philosophiae partes penitus **hausisse**; neque iis doctoribus contentum, quorum ei copia in urbe contigerat, Achaiam quoque et Asiam **peragrasse**, ut[12] omnem omnium artium varietatem complecteretur. itaque hercule in libris Ciceronis deprehendere licet non geometriae, non musicae, non grammaticae, non denique ullius ingenuae artis **scientiam** ei **defuisse**. ille dialecticae subtilitatem, ille moralis partis utilitatem, ille rerum motus causasque cognoverat. ita est enim, optimi viri, ita est: ex multa eruditione et plurimis artibus et omnium rerum scientia exundat et exuberat illa admirabilis eloquentia. Tacitus, *Dialogus*

---

[12] *ut*: 'so that (he) might...'.

Exercise 1E: Indirect Commands (i)

a) mihi persuasit ut tecum loquerer.
b) te precor, Iuppiter, ut ventos secundos des.
c) per deos vos, milites, oro et obsecro ne stationem relinquatis.
d) Hector Aenean monuit ut sine mora Ilio decederet neve in arma rueret.
e) Iason Argonautas hortabatur ut remis incumberent.
f) praefectus nautis imperabat ut ventis vela intenderent.
g) Anna sorori suadere frustra conatur ne in gladium incidat.
h) vir uxori imperavit ut taceret neu latronibus genus familiamque indicaret.
i) pecunia multa multis persuadet ut facinora nefaria faciant.
j) Caesar milites adhortabatur ut barbaris omni virtute praestarent.

Exercise 1F: Indirect Commands (ii)

Legates make terms with Hannibal.

legati ad Hannibalem uenerunt pacemque cum eo condicionibus fecerunt **ne** quis imperator magistratusue Poenorum ius ullum in ciuem Campanum **haberet neue** ciuis Campanus inuitus **militaret** munusue **faceret**; **ut** suae leges, sui magistratus Capuae **essent**; **ut** trecentos ex Romanis captiuis Poenus **daret** Campanis, quos ipsi elegissent, cum quibus equitum Campanorum, qui in Sicilia stipendia facerent, permutatio fieret. haec pacta. illa insuper quam pacta erant facinora Campani ediderunt: nam praefectos socium ciuesque Romanos alios, partim aliquo militiae munere occupatos, partim priuatis negotiis implicitos, plebs repente omnes comprehensos uelut custodiae causa balneis includi iussit, ubi[13] feruore atque aestu anima interclusa foedum in modum exspirarent. Livy

[13] *ubi*: 'where they might…'

Exercise 1G[V]: Indirect Questions (i)

a) nescio cur iste liberos illos laudaverit.
b) rogavere quales libros legere soleres.
c) nusquam apparet unde arcus pluvius oriatur.
d) nemo recordari poterat a quo principio seditio orsa esset.
e) cognoscere omnes volebamus num hostes conspicati essent necne.
f) socii nesciunt quibus dis hostias dux Romanus immolet.
g) Troiani serius comperiebant quantos dolos Graeci paravissent.
h) commota dolore Althaea dicere non poterat quare filium suum necasset.
i) audite, iudices, quantum scelus hic reus turpissime fecerit!
j) nemo certo scit qua ex re Caesar Nasonem e patria expulerit.

Exercise 1H: Indirect Questions (ii)

The poet asks Erato for inspiration in his song.

nunc age, **qui** reges, Erato, **quae** tempora, rerum
quis Latio antiquo **fuerit** status, advena[14] classem
cum primum Ausoniis exercitus appulit oris,
expediam, et primae revocabo exordia pugnae.
tu vatem, tu, diva, mone. dicam horrida bella,
dicam acies actosque animis in funera reges,
Tyrrhenamque manum totamque sub arma coactam
Hesperiam. maior rerum mihi nascitur ordo,
maius opus moveo.

Virgil, *Aeneid*

---

[14] *advena*: this noun is in apposition to *exercitus*; translate as an adjective, 'foreign army'.

Exercise 1J: Mixed Indirect Speech

a) hoc signum nos monet ut canem caveamus neve domum intremus.
b) medicus nesciebat utrum infans gravi morbo aeger victurus esset necne.
c) pater iratus filium rogitabat quo tam mane iisset.
d) dic mihi cui pecuniam dederis.
e) reus ab iudicibus petiit ut misericordiam misero adhiberent neve liberos miserrimos patre privarent.
f) Clodius iuveni persuasit ut plus meri quam deceret potaret.
g) Cicero ab indicibus certior fiebat Catilinam conspirationem parare.
h) Daedalus Icarum monuit ne propius ad solem volaret.
i) fama Romam celeriter perlata est multos, inter quos etiam mulieres liberique essent, crudelissime trucidatos esse.
j) Cicero prae se ferebat se patriam ex tanto periculo servasse.

Exercises for Level Two

Exercise 2A

The philosophy of Zeno, the founding father of Stoicism.[15]

fuit enim quidam summo ingenio vir, Zeno, cuius inventorum aemuli Stoici nominantur. huius sententiae sunt et praecepta eius modi: **sapientem** gratia numquam **moveri**, numquam cuiusquam delicto **ignoscere**; **neminem** misericordem **esse** nisi stultum et levem; viri[16] non **esse** neque[17] exorari neque placari;...**nos** autem, qui sapientes non sumus, fugitivos, exsules, hostes, insanos denique **esse** dicunt; **omnia peccata esse** paria; **omne delictum** scelus **esse** nefarium, nec minus **delinquere eum**, qui gallum gallinaceum,[18] cum opus non fuerit, quam eum, qui patrem suffocaverit; **sapientem** nihil **opinari**, nullius rei **paenitere**, nulla in re **falli**, sententiam **mutare** numquam.

Cicero, *Pro Murena*

---

[15] Students with no previous knowledge of Stoicism might find it helpful to consult the *Oxford Classical Dictionary* under 'Stoa', or another similar reference manual, before translating.

[16] *viri non esse*: a genitive of characteristic, for which see the **Glossary of Technical Terms**.

[17] *neque...neque...*: these negatives reinforce the first negative *non*, rather than cancelling them out. Translate 'either…or…'.

[18] *qui gallum gallinaceum*: for the verb of this clause supply *suffocaverit* from the following *qui*-clause.

Exercise 2B

Jugurtha encourages his troops before battle.

igitur in eo colle...Iugurtha extenuata suorum acie consedit. elephantis et parti copiarum pedestrium Bomilcarem praefecit eumque edocet quae ageret.[19] ipse propior montem cum omni equitatu et peditibus delectis suos conlocat. dein singulas turmas et manipulos circumiens monet atque obtestatur, **uti** memores pristinae virtutis et victoriae sese regnumque suom ab Romanorum avaritia **defendant**: cum iis **certamen fore**, quos antea victos sub iugum miserint; **ducem** illis, non **animum mutatum**; quae ab imperatore decuerint **omnia** suis **provisa, locum superiorem**, ut[20] prudentes cum inperitis, ne pauciores cum pluribus aut rudes cum belli melioribus manum consererent; proinde parati intentique **essent** signo dato Romanos invadere: **illum diem** aut omnis labores et victorias **confirmaturum** aut maxumarum aerumnarum initium **fore**. Sallust, *Bellum Iugurthinum*

Exercise 2C

Seek out the right girl while you are able.

dum licet et loris passim potes ire solutis,
    elige **cui dicas** 'tu mihi sola places.'
haec tibi non tenues ueniet delapsa per auras;
    quaerenda est oculis apta puella tuis.[21]
scit bene uenator, ceruis **ubi** retia **tendat**;
    scit bene, **qua** frendens ualle **moretur** aper;
aucupibus noti frutices; qui sustinet hamos,
    nouit **quae** multo pisce **natentur** aquae:
tu quoque, materiam longo qui quaeris amori,
    ante frequens **quo sit** disce puella loco.[22] Ovid, *Ars Am.*

---

[19] *Quae ageret*: 'what he was to do'.
[20] *ut...ne*: see **6. Purpose and Result Clauses Part 1 B** i).
[21] *quaerenda est oculis...tuis*: see **5. Gerunds and Gerundives D** a).
[22] *ante frequens...loco*: take in the following order, *disce quo loco puella sit ante frequens*.

Exercises for Level Three

Exercise 3A

Caesar receives information from the Ubii about the activity of the Suebi.

interim paucis post diebus fit[23] ab Ubiis certior **Suebos omnis** in unum locum copias **cogere** atque eis nationibus quae sub eorum sint imperio **denuntiare ut** auxilia peditatus equitatusque **mittant**. His cognitis rebus, rem frumentariam providet, castris idoneum locum deligit; Ubiis imperat **ut** pecora **deducant** suaque omnia ex agris in oppida **conferant**, sperans **barbaros atque imperitos homines** inopia cibariorum adductos ad iniquam pugnandi[24] condicionem **posse** deduci; mandat **ut** crebros exploratores in Suebos **mittant quae**que apud eos **gerantur cognoscant**. Illi imperata faciunt et paucis diebus intermissis referunt: **Suebos omnis**, postea quam certiores nuntii de exercitu Romanorum venerint, cum omnibus suis sociorumque copiis quas coegissent penitus ad extremos finis sese **recepisse**: **silvam esse** ibi infinita magnitudine, quae appellatur Bacenis; **hanc** longe introrsus **pertinere** et pro nativo muro obiectam Cheruscos ab Suebis Suebosque ab Cheruscis iniuriis incursionibusque **prohibere**: ad eius initium silvae **Suebos** adventum Romanorum exspectare **constituisse**.

Caesar, *Bellum Gallicum*

---

[23] The subject is *Caesar*.

[24] *pugnandi*: see **5. Gerunds and Gerundives D** c).

Exercise 3B

Pythagoras and Sextius had different reasons for vegetarianism.

quoniam coepi tibi exponere **quanto maiore impetu** ad philosophiam iuuenis **accesserim** quam senex **pergam**, non pudebit fateri **quem** mihi **amorem** Pythagoras **iniecerit**. Sotion dicebat **quare** ille animalibus **abstinuisset**, **quare** postea Sextius. dissimilis utrique causa erat, sed utrique magnifica. hic homini **satis** alimentorum citra sanguinem **esse** credebat, et crudelitatis **consuetudinem fieri** ubi in uoluptatem esset adducta laceratio. adiciebat contrahendam[25] **materiam esse** luxuriae. colligebat bonae ualitudini contraria **esse alimenta uaria** et nostris aliena corporibus. at Pythagoras omnium inter omnia **cognationem esse** dicebat et animorum **commercium** in alias atque alias formas transeuntium. nulla, si illi credas[26], anima interit, ne cessat quidem nisi tempore exiguo, dum in aliud corpus transfunditur. uidebimus **per quas** temporum **uices** et **quando** pererratis pluribus domiciliis in hominem **reuertatur**: interim sceleris hominibus ac parricidii metum fecit, cum possent[27] in parentis animam inscii incurrere et ferro morsuue uiolare, si in quo cognatus aliqui spiritus hospitaretur[28].

Seneca, *Letters*

---

[25] *contrahendam...esse*: see **5. Gerunds and Gerundives D** b) i).
[26] *si illi credas*: see **9. Conditional Sentences C** i).
[27] *cum possent*: see **4. Temporal Conjunctions E** vi).
[28] *si...hospitaretur*: see **9. Conditional Sentences C** ii).

Exercise 3C

Ariadne is distraught at Theseus' faithlessness.

sed quid ego a primo digressus carmine plura
commemorem,[29] **ut** linquens genitoris filia uultum,
ut consanguineae complexum, **ut** denique matris,
quae misera in gnata deperdita laetabatur,[30]
omnibus his Thesei dulcem **praeoptarit** amorem:
aut **ut** uecta rati spumosa ad litora Diae
uenerit, aut **ut** eam deuinctam lumina[31] somno
liquerit immemori discedens pectore coniunx?
saepe **illam** perhibent ardenti corde furentem
clarisonas imo **fudisse** e pectore uoces,
ac tum praeruptos tristem **conscendere** montes,
unde aciem in pelagi uastos protenderet aestus,
tum tremuli salis aduersas **procurrere** in undas
mollia nudatae tollentem tegmina surae,
atque haec extremis maestam **dixisse** querellis,
frigidulos udo singultus ore cientem:
'sicine me patriis auectam, perfide, ab aris,
perfide, deserto liquisti in litore, Theseu?'

Catullus

---

[29] See **8. Independent Subjunctives C.**

[30] *deperdita*: 'dying with love'.

[31] *deuinctam lumina*: *lumina* is an accusative of respect, for which see the **Glossary of Technical Terms.**

Exercises for Level Four

Exercise 4A

Reactions to the threat on Plautus' life.

Plauto **parari necem** non perinde occultum fuit, quia pluribus salus eius curabatur et spatium itineris ac maris tempusque interiectum mouerat famam; uulgoque fingebant **petitum** ab eo **Corbulonem**, magnis tum exercitibus praesidentem et, clari atque insontes si interficerentur, **praecipuum** ad pericula. quin et **Asiam** fauore iuuenis arma **cepisse**, nec **milites** ad scelus missos aut numero ualidos aut animo promptos, postquam iussa efficere nequiuerint, ad spes nouas **transisse**. uana haec more famae credentium otio augebantur; ceterum libertus Plauti celeritate uentorum praeuenit centurionem et mandata L. Antistii soceri attulit: **effugeret** segnem mortem, dum suffugium esset: magni nominis miseratione **reperturum** bonos, **consociaturum** audacis: **nullum** interim **subsidium aspernandum**. si sexaginta milites (tot enim adueniebant) propulisset, dum refertur nuntius Neroni, dum manus alia permeat, **multa secutura** quae adusque bellum eualescerent. denique aut **salutem** tali consilio **quaeri**, aut **nihil** grauius audenti quam ignauo **patiendum esse**.

Tacitus, *Annals*

Exercise 4B

'Wisdom is the beginning and source of writing well.'

ergo fungar vice cotis, acutum
reddere quae ferrum valet exsors ipsa secandi;
munus et officium nil scribens ipse docebo,
unde parentur opes, **quid alat formetque** poetam,
quid deceat, **quid** non, **quo** virtus, **quo ferat** error.
scribendi recte sapere est et principium et fons:
rem tibi Socraticae poterunt ostendere chartae,
verbaque provisam rem non invita sequentur.
qui didicit, patriae **quid debeat** et **quid** amicis,
quo sit amore parens, **quo** frater amandus et hospes,
quod sit conscripti, **quod** iudicis officium, **quae**
partes in bellum missi ducis, ille profecto
reddere personae scit convenientia cuique.
respicere exemplar vitae morumque iubebo
doctum imitatorem et vivas hinc ducere voces.
interdum speciosa locis morataque recte
fabula nullius veneris, sine pondere et arte,
valdius oblectat populum meliusque moratur
quam versus inopes rerum nugaeque canorae.

Horace, *Ars Poetica*

Chapter 3

PREDICATIVE DATIVES

Parallel Revision: Forms of Nouns, Kennedy 34-57, CLG 1, OLG pp. 16-17.

A. What is a Predicative Dative?

In essence, a simple sentence consists of two basic elements, a subject and the predicate. The subject is indicated in Latin by the use of the nominative case.[1] The term 'predicate' denotes the remaining part of the sentence, i.e. the part which describes the action or state of the subject. Since this predicate describes the *action* or *state* of the subject, it must contain a verb. When the verb indicating the *state* of the subject is the verb 'to be', the predicate is normally completed by a complement, shown in the same case as the subject, i.e. the nominative:[2]

Subject	Predicate
Cicero	was a 'new man'.
Cicero	*novus homo erat.*
The republic	is glorious.
respublica	*gloriosa est.*

However, when the state described by the complement is an abstract quality, e.g. qualities such as 'help', 'hindrance', 'destruction', 'pleasure', 'concern', etc., a dative is often used in place of this nominative[3] complement of the verb 'to be'.

[1] This statement is valid for all subjects in direct speech; in indirect speech, of course, the subject is indicated by the accusative case. See **2. Indirect Speech Part 2 A** i).

[2] Compare note 1 above.

[3] The accusative in indirect statements.

So, for example, instead of *auxilium est* 'He is a help', Latin frequently uses *auxilio est*; in place of *impedimentum est* 'He is a hindrance', we find *impedimento est*. This dative is called a *predicative* dative.

B. How do we translate a predicative dative?

The difference in sense created by the use of this predicative dative in place of the nominative complement seems largely to be one of nuance. The dative perhaps highlights the fact that the subject is not in itself the embodiment of these abstract qualities, but represents this quality in the situation described. Since this difference in sense is so minimal, it is often possible to translate the dative as though it were simply a nominative complement, as, for example, in the examples given above: *auxilio est* 'He is a help'; *impedimento est* 'He is a hindrance'.

At other times, however, translation in this way produces a very stilted result: for example,

exitio est 'He is a destruction';

detrimento est 'He is a detriment'.

In these situations, a more fluent translation may often be created by using a related adjective or verb in place of the predicative dative:

exitio est 'He destroys'/ 'He is destructive';

detrimento est 'He is detrimental to'.

For a more complete guide to translation, see the table of **Common Predicative Dative Expressions** below.

C. How do we recognise a predicative dative?

There are two features of the predicative dative which make it easy to recognise:

i) The number of abstract qualities which appear as part of predicative dative expressions is fairly limited. Those predicative dative expressions which do exist, however, tend

to be very common. In one sense, therefore, predicative dative expressions can be said to be formulaic, since the same expressions occur over and over again. A list of these common predicative dative expressions is provided below.
ii) The person to whom 'one is a help' or to whom 'one is a hindrance (etc.)' is often (but not always) expressed by a second dative. The predicative dative can therefore often be recognised by the presence of two *nouns* in the dative dependent on some form of the verb 'to be'.

D. Common Predicative Dative Expressions

Predicative Dative	Literal Translation	Possible Translation
impedimento sum	'I am a hindrance to…'	'I hinder…'
exitio sum	'I am a destruction to…'	'I destroy…'
detrimento sum	'I am a detriment to…'	'I am detrimental to…'
dolori sum	'I am a cause of grief to…'	'I cause grief for…'
odio sum	'I am an object of hatred to…'	'I am hated by/odious to…'
saluti sum	'I am a source of safety for…'	'I save…'
adiumento sum	'I am a help to…'	'I help…/am helpful to…'
auxilio sum	'I am a help to…'	'I help…/am helpful to…'
cordi sum	'I am dear to…'	(as literal)
curae sum	'I am an object of concern /care to…'	'I am taken care of/loved by…'
voluptati sum	'I am a source of pleasure for…'	'I give pleasure to…'
bono sum	'I am an advantage to…'	'I am advantageous to…'
gloriae sum	'I am a source of glory to…'	(as literal)

honori sum	'I am a source of honour to...'	(as literal)
decori sum	'I am a source of honour to...'	(as literal)
pudori sum	'I am a source of shame to...	'I am shameful to...'
dedecori sum	'I am a source of dishonour to...'	(as literal)
opprobrio sum	'I am a disgrace to...'	(as literal)
spectaculo sum	'I am a spectacle to...'	(as literal)
usui sum	'I am a use to...'	'I am of use to...'
oneri sum	'I am a burden to...'	(as literal)
argumento sum	'I am a proof to...'	(as literal)
morae sum	'I am a cause of delay to...'	'I delay...'

E. The predicative dative with other verbs

A dative occasionally takes the place of an *accusative* noun or adjective after the verbs:

i) *habeo* or *duco*, when used in the sense of 'I consider';

ii) *do* or *verto*, when used in the sense of 'I ascribe'.

This means that instead of *habeo aliquid quaestum* to express 'I consider something a source of gain' Latin uses *habeo aliquid quaestui*. As with predicative datives after *sum*, the predicative dative after the verbs listed above is limited to a small number of common expressions:

Predicative Dative	Literal Translation	Possible Translation
quaestui habeo	'I consider x (acc.) as a source of gain'	'I consider x (acc.) profitable'
vitio do/verto	'I ascribe x (acc.) as a fault'	(as literal)
probro duco/habeo	'I consider x (acc.) as a subject for reproach'	'I consider x (acc.) disgraceful'
laudi do	'I ascribe x (acc.) as a cause of praise'	'I ascribe x (acc.) as a reason for praising'

Exercises for Level One

Exercise 1A

a) Io magnae curae Iovi est.
b) discordia civilis civibus bonis odio est.
c) nemo parentibus suis dolori esse vult.
d) Zeno luxuriam magnam summo bono maximo detrimento esse credebat.
e) aliqui opinantur divitias haud aliud quam mortalibus oneri esse.
f) Pharos nautis saluti est.
g) fuga dedecori magno militibus fortibus semper erit.
h) ille servus in crucem actus exemplo omnibus aliis furibus erat.
i) recitationes voluptati hominibus doctissimis atque humanissimis sunt.
j) constat genus nobile candidatis bono esse.

Exercise 1B (i)

Self-indulgence creates worthless men.

['Men's achievements in ploughing, sailing and building all depend upon virtue...']

sed multi mortales, dediti ventri atque somno, indocti incultique vitam sicuti peregrinantes transigere;[4] **quibus** profecto contra naturam corpus **voluptati**, anima **oneri fuit**. eorum ego vitam mortemque iuxta aestumo, quoniam de utraque siletur. verum enim vero is demum mihi vivere atque frui anima videtur, qui aliquo negotio intentus praeclari facinoris aut artis bonae famam quaerit.

Sallust, *Catilinae Coniuratio*

---

[4] *transigere*: a historic infinitive, for which see the **Glossary of Technical Terms**.

Exercise 1B (ii)

Love of money and power were the cause of all evils.

sed ubi labore atque iustitia res publica crevit, reges magni bello domiti, nationes ferae et populi ingentes vi subacti, Carthago aemula imperi Romani ab stirpe interiit, cuncta maria terraeque patebant, saevire fortuna ac miscere omnia coepit. qui labores, pericula, dubias atque asperas res facile toleraverant, **iis** otium divitiaeque, optanda[5] alias, **oneri miseriaeque fuere**. igitur primo pecuniae, deinde imperi cupido crevit: ea quasi materies omnium malorum fuere.

Sallust, *Catilinae Coniuratio*

Exercise 1B (iii)

The love of riches brought about a decline in virtue.

postquam divitiae **honori esse** coepere et eas gloria imperium potentia sequebatur, hebescere virtus, paupertas **probro haberi**, innocentia pro malevolentia duci coepit. igitur ex divitiis iuventutem luxuria atque avaritia cum superbia invasere: rapere[6] consumere, sua parvi[7] pendere, aliena cupere; pudorem pudicitiam, divina atque humana promiscua, nihil pensi neque moderati habere.[8]

Sallust, *Catilinae Coniuratio*

---

[5] *optanda*: 'desirable'.

[6] *rapere consumere...pendere etc.*: historic infinitives, for which see the **Glossary of Technical Terms.**

[7] *parvi...pensi*: genitives of value, for which see the **Glossary of Technical Terms.**

[8] *nihil pensi neque moderati habere*: 'they neither valued nor controlled'.

Exercises for Level Two

Exercise 2A

a) vitis ut arboribus decori est, ut vitibus uvae,
ut gregibus tauri, segetes ut pinguibus arvis,
tu decus omne tuis. (Virgil)

b) habere quaestui rempublicam nefarium est. (Cicero)

c) pluma tegit volucres, ovibus sua lana decori est. (Ovid)

d) virginibus cordi grataque forma sua est. (Ovid)

e) estne novis nuptis odio Venus? (Catullus)

f) nil nisi turpe iuvat; curae sua cuique voluptas. (Ovid)

g) [haec] nos vero arbitramur non modo nullo adiumento esse, sed potius maximo impedimento. (*Ad Herennium*)

h) ad vos confugi, patres conscripti, quibus...cogor prius oneri quam usui esse. (Sallust)

i) genus Fabium insigne spectaculo exemploque civibus erat. (Livy)

j) reperies... multis insitam opinionem non initia nostri, non finem, non denique homines dis curae. (Tacitus)

Exercise 2B (i)

Catullus is unimpressed by Iuventius' choice of lover.

nemone in tanto potuit populo esse, Iuuenti,
    bellus homo, quem tu diligere inciperes,[9]
praeterquam iste tuus moribunda ab sede Pisauri
    hospes inaurata pallidior statua,
qui **tibi** nunc **cordi est**, quem tu praeponere nobis
    audes, et nescis quod facinus facias?[10]

Catullus

[9] *inciperes*: for the subjunctive, see **6. Purpose and Result Clauses Part 2 B**.
[10] *facias*: see **2. Indirect Speech Part 6**.

Exercise 2B (ii)

There is good precedent for loving a slave-girl.

ne[11] **sit** ancillae **tibi** amor **pudori**,
Xanthia Phoceu, prius insolentem
serva Briseis niveo colore
    movit Achillem;
movit Aiacem Telamone natum
forma captivae dominum Tecmessae;
arsit Atrides medio in triumpho
    virgine rapta,
barbarae postquam cecidere turmae
Thessalo victore et ademptus Hector
tradidit fessis leviora tolli
    Pergama Grais.

Horace, *Odes*

[11] *ne*: see **6. Purpose and Result Clauses Part 1 B** i).

Exercises for Level Three

Exercise 3A

Memmius is discouraged by the power of the 'enemy' at home.

'multa me dehortantur a vobis, Quirites, ni studium rei publicae omnia superet:[12] opes factionis, vostra patientia, ius nullum, ac maxume quod innocentiae plus periculi quam honoris est. nam illa quidem piget dicere, his annis quindecim quam **ludibrio** fueritis superbiae paucorum, quam foede quamque inulti perierint vostri defensores, ut[13] vobis animus ab ignavia atque socordia conruptus sit, qui ne nunc quidem obnoxiis inimicis exurgitis atque etiam nunc timetis eos, quibus decet **terrori** esse...superioribus annis taciti indignabamini aerarium expilari, reges et populos liberos paucis nobilibus vectigal pendere, penes eosdem et summam gloriam et maxumas divitias esse. tamen haec talia facinora inpune suscepisse parum habuere, itaque postremo leges, maiestas vostra, divina et humana omnia hostibus tradita sunt. neque eos qui ea fecere pudet aut paenitet, sed incedunt per ora vostra magnifici, sacerdotia et consulatus, pars triumphos suos ostentantes; proinde quasi ea **honori**, non **praedae** habeant. servi aere parati iniusta imperia dominorum non perferunt; vos, Quirites, in imperio nati aequo animo servitutem toleratis? at qui sunt ii, qui rem publicam occupavere? homines sceleratissumi, cruentis manibus, immani avaritia, nocentissumi et idem superbissumi, quibus fides decus pietas, postremo honesta atque inhonesta omnia **quaestui** sunt.

Sallust, *Bellum Iugurthinum*

---

[12] *ni...superet*: see **9. Conditional Sentences E** ii).

[13] *ut...conruptus sit*: see **6. Purpose and Result Clauses Part 2 A.**

Exercise 3B

Jupiter's plan to destroy the world grieves the lesser gods.

dicta Iovis pars voce probant stimulosque frementi
adiciunt, alii partes adsensibus implent.
est tamen humani generis iactura **dolori**
omnibus, et quae sit terrae mortalibus orbae
forma futura rogant, quis sit laturus in aras
tura, ferisne paret populandas[14] tradere terras.
talia quaerentes (**sibi** enim **fore** cetera **curae**)[15]
rex superum trepidare vetat subolemque priori
dissimilem populo promittit origine mira.
iamque erat in totas sparsurus fulmina terras;
sed timuit, ne[16] forte sacer tot ab ignibus aether
conciperet flammas longusque ardesceret axis:
esse quoque in fatis reminiscitur, adfore tempus,
quo mare, quo tellus correptaque regia caeli
ardeat et mundi moles obsessa laboret.
tela reponuntur manibus fabricata cyclopum;
poena placet diversa, genus mortale sub undis
perdere et ex omni nimbos demittere caelo.

Ovid, *Metamorphoses*

---

[14] *populandas*: see **5. Gerunds and Gerundives D** b) v).

[15] To this parenthesis add an introductory verb of speaking, e.g. 'For he said that...'.

[16] *timuit, ne*...: see **7. Verbs of Fearing/*quominus* & *quin* Part 1**.

Exercise for Level Four

Exercise 4A

'What is honourable and what is shameful is not the same in the eyes of all.'

non dubito fore plerosque, Attice, qui hoc genus scripturae leue et non satis dignum summorum uirorum personis iudicent, cum relatum legent, quis musicam docuerit Epaminondam, aut in eius uirtutibus commemorari, saltasse eum commode scienterque tibiis cantasse. sed ii erunt fere, qui expertes litterarum Graecarum nihil rectum, nisi quod ipsorum moribus conueniat, putabunt. hi si didicerint non eadem omnibus esse honesta atque turpia, sed omnia maiorum institutis iudicari, non admirabuntur nos in Graiorum uirtutibus exponendis mores eorum secutos. neque enim Cimoni fuit turpe, Atheniensium summo uiro, sororem germanam habere in matrimonio, quippe cum ciues eius eodem uterentur instituto. at id quidem nostris moribus nefas habetur. **laudi** in Creta **ducitur adulescentulis** quam plurimos habuisse amatores. nulla Lacedaemoni uidua tam est nobilis, quae non ad cenam eat mercede conducta. magnis in laudibus tota fere fuit Graecia uictorem Olympiae citari, in scaenam uero prodire ac **populo esse spectaculo nemini** in eisdem gentibus **fuit turpitudini**. quae omnia apud nos partim infamia, partim humilia atque ab honestate remota ponuntur.

Cornelius Nepos

Chapter 4

TEMPORAL CONJUNCTIONS

Parallel Revision: Present, Future and Imperfect Indicatives of Active, Passive, Deponent and Irregular Verbs, Kennedy 115-25, 133-41, CLG 7b-7c, 8a, 9.1, OLG pp. 36-62.

A. What are Temporal Conjunctions?

Temporal conjunctions are words that introduce clauses related to **time**, e.g. 'after', 'when', 'before', 'until' etc., as in:

'*After* their parents had left, the children relaxed.'

'*When* he had said all that he wanted, he fell silent.'

'*Before* he went, he bade farewell to all his friends.'

Occasionally, temporal conjunctions are required to introduce clauses expressing more than just time, as, for example, in the sentence

'The soldier fled, *before* he *could* be taken captive.'

Here, the temporal conjunction 'before' introduces a subordinate clause indicating not only the *time* at which the soldier fled, but also his *purpose* in fleeing. **Purpose**, therefore, is sometimes indicated in the context of temporal clauses. Similarly, temporal clauses may also express the idea of **expectation** in addition to time, as in:

'He waited *until* he *might* lay his hands on that inheritance'.

B. Temporal Conjunctions in Latin

i) Most temporal conjunctions in Latin observe the following general rules:

- when expressing **time** alone, they use the **indicative** mood;
- when conveying **time linked with purpose or expectation**, they use the **subjunctive**.[1]

ii) In practice, the sense of some temporal conjunctions, e.g. 'when', 'after', is such that they are *only* required to indicate the **time** at which something happened, with no added sense of purpose or expectation. These conjunctions are followed by the **indicative** (see section **C** below), *except* when the clause occurs within indirect speech, when they will usually be followed by a subjunctive verb to show that they belong to the words being reported (see **2. Indirect Speech Part 4 E**).

iii) Conjunctions meaning 'until' and 'before' are frequently followed by verbs which discriminate between 'time alone' and 'time linked with purpose or expectation', by using the indicative and the subjunctive respectively.[2]

iv) Two conjunctions, *dum* and *cum*, have a wide variety of specific uses, which do not conform to the above rule and which must therefore be *learnt*.

---

[1] This distinction between the use of the indicative and the subjunctive with temporal conjunctions becomes blurred in texts from Livy onwards, when the subjunctive is used more indiscriminately, without necessarily indicating any added sense of purpose or expectation.

[2] Within indirect speech, however, for the reason indicated above in ii), that it is the norm for subordinate clauses to take a subjunctive verb (see **2. Indirect Speech Part 4 E**), this distinction cannot be made. In indirect speech, therefore, it is wise to assume that all temporal conjunctions indicate 'time alone', unless there are very strong reasons for believing otherwise.

C. Temporal conjunctions which most commonly take the Indicative:

Temporal Conjunctions	Translation
ubi, ut, quando	'when'
postquam	'after'
simul ac/atque, cum primum	'as soon as'
quotiens	'as often as'
quamdiu, donec, quoad	'as long as'

Latin idiom often differs from English with respect to tenses. After conjunctions meaning 'when', 'after' and 'as soon as', where Latin uses a perfect tense, English prefers the pluperfect. Translate accordingly:

> *postquam patronum salutaverunt* (**perfect** indicative), *clientes sportulam accepere.*
> 'After they *had* greeted their patron, the clients received their food-baskets'.

D. Temporal conjunctions which take either the indicative or the subjunctive:

Temporal Conjunction	With Indicative	With Subjunctive
donec, quoad	'until x happens'	'until x might/could should happen' (rare)
antequam, priusquam	'before x happens'	'before x might/could happen'

So,

> *fur clam egressus est antequam quisquam se conspicatus est.*

using the **indicative** after *antequam* means

> 'The thief left furtively before anyone saw him.'

and so refers only to the **time** at which he left, whereas

fur clam egressus est antequam quisquam se conspicaretur.

using the **subjunctive** after *antequam* means

'The thief left furtively before anyone *could* see him.'

and indicates his **purpose** in leaving, in addition to the time.

E. cum[3]

i) *cum* takes both an indicative and a subjunctive verb, but the distinction between the usage of the two moods is *not* one of 'time alone' as opposed to 'purpose-expectation'.

ii) With the **indicative** *cum* most commonly means '**when**':

cum seniores erimus, sapientiores erimus.

'**When** we are older, we shall be wiser.'

This illustration again reveals a difference of preference in the use of tenses: Latin uses a future indicative in the *cum*-clause to indicate (accurately) that the situation described is still to happen, whereas English (less accurately) uses the present. After observing carefully the tense of the Latin verb, allow your instinct to guide your choice of tense in English.

iii) When the **indicative** used with *cum* is a **past tense**, instead of 'when', it *may* (but does not always) mean '**whenever**'. When *cum* is followed by a past tense of the indicative, then, it is necessary to bear this alternative meaning in mind and to allow the context to dictate which is the most appropriate option. English idiom again differs from Latin with respect to the tenses used with *cum* meaning 'whenever': where Latin uses a perfect indicative, English

[3] Do not confuse the temporal conjunction *cum* with the preposition *cum* 'with', which is followed by a noun or pronoun in the ablative case.

prefers the present tense and where Latin uses a pluperfect, English prefers the perfect. Observe this difference in preference in your translation:

> *cum filius mentitus erat* (**pluperfect** indicative), *matrem haudquaquam fallebat.*
>
> '*Whenever* the son *lied*, his mother did not fail to notice.'

iv) *cum* followed by the **indicative** and meaning '**when**' sometimes introduces a so-called *cum inversum* (or 'inverted *cum*') clause. This occurs when the *cum*-clause contains the most important idea in the sentence, even though grammatically it is subordinate to the main clause. For example, in the sentence

> 'The messenger was returning to his camp, when he fell into an ambush.'

'he fell into an ambush' expresses the most important idea of the sentence, although *grammatically* it is subordinate to 'The messenger was returning to his camp'. Since, as illustrated by this example, the English language exhibits the same phenomenon as Latin, no difficulty should occur in translation. *cum inversum* clauses are usually found in the context of dramatic or surprise happenings. The use of an indicative in a past (or historic present) tense is also common:

> *talia vociferans gemitu tectum omne replebat,*
> *cum subitum dictuque oritur mirabile monstrum...*
>
> (Virgil)
>
> 'Saying these words, she filled the entire house with her groaning, *when* suddenly a portent, amazing to speak of, occurred...'.

v) With a **present subjunctive**[4] *cum* means '**since**' or '**although**'. Where *cum* with the present subjunctive means

---

[4] Very occasionally, *cum* followed by the perfect subjunctive also has this meaning.

'although', the main clause will often contain either *tamen* 'however' or *nihilominus* 'nevertheless'; similarly, where *cum* with the subjunctive means 'since', the main clause often contains *praesertim* 'especially' or occasionally *quippe* 'of course':

> *cum iuvenes ignavissimi saepius habeantur, re tamen vera multi doctrinarum studiosissimi sunt.*
>
> '**Although** youngsters are more often considered very idle, in reality, however, many are extremely studious in their learning.'

vi) With the **imperfect** or **pluperfect subjunctive** *cum* means either '**when**' or '**since**' or '**although**'. Only the context can indicate which choice of translation is most appropriate; as above, however, *cum* meaning 'although' is often suggested by the presence of a *tamen* or *nihilominus* in the main clause and *cum* meaning 'since' may be indicated by the presence of *praesertim*:

> *cum litteras perlegisset, sine responso nuntium dimisit.*
>
> '**When** he had read the letter all the way through, he sent the messenger away without a reply.'
>
> *cum mihi tam bene faceres, tibi maximas gratias ago.*
>
> '**Since** you were so kind to me, I thank you most wholeheartedly.'
>
> *cum ille eam non amaret, orbam nihilominus domum duxit.*
>
> '**Although** he did not love her, *nevertheless* he married the orphaned girl.'

vii) A clause or phrase beginning with *cum* is sometimes followed by a clause or phrase beginning with *tum*. Depending on the context, suitable translations for *cum...tum...* include '**not only...but also...**', '**both... and...** ' and '**although... yet...** '.

vir cum clarissimus tum vero optimus mihique amicissimus... (Cicero)
'a man who was not only very famous but also most excellent and most friendly to me...'

F. dum

dum may mean either '**while** x was happening/happened', '**as long as**', '**until**' or '**provided that**'.

i) *dum* meaning '**while** x was happening/happened' is found with a **present indicative**:

dum carmen vates canit, omnes tacebant.
'While the poet sang his song, everyone was silent.'

ii) *dum* meaning '**as long as**' is found with an **indicative** in **any** appropriate **tense**.

dum vires mihi supererunt, maximam tuam virtutem memorabo.
'As long as my strength remains (lit. shall remain), I shall speak of your very great courage.'

iii) *dum* meaning '**until**' is found with **either** an **indicative or subjunctive**. The distinction between the use of the indicative and the subjunctive is the same as that described above for the majority of temporal conjunctions, namely that the **indicative** indicates **time alone**, whereas the **subjunctive** indicates **purpose/expectation** in addition to time:

classis praefectus Brindisi morabatur dum mandata recentia accepit.
'The captain of the fleet delayed at Brundisium until he received fresh instructions.'

classis praefectus Brindisi morabatur dum ventis secundis navigaret.
'The captain of the fleet delayed at Brundisium until he could set sail with favourable winds.'

iv) *dum* meaning '**provided that**' is found with a **subjunctive**; in this sense *dum* is often strengthened by the addition of *modo*, printed either as a separate word or as a suffix.[5] No additional word need be sought for *modo* in translation. When a negative is required in a *dum*-clause of this type, *ne* is used. The presence of a *ne* in a *dum*-clause is therefore an indication in itself that the appropriate translation of *dum* is 'provided that':

dum satis pecuniae sit, tibi licet quidlibet emere.
'Provided that you have (lit. there is) enough money, you may buy whatever you like.'
dummodo nimis clamoris ne faciatis, vobis licet foris ludere.
'Provided that you do not make too much noise, you may play outdoors.'

---

[5] *modo* on its own with the subjunctive is also found in this sense.

Exercises for Level One

Exercise 1A[V]

This exercise concentrates on temporal conjunctions which take either the indicative or the subjunctive, cum and dum.

a) victi se dedidere priusquam occiderentur.
b) multi se in fugam dederunt antequam agmen barbarum ad urbem pervenit.
c) quae cum ita sint, reum poenas mortis dare oportet.
d) cum res ita se haberent, senatus tamen exercitum in Italiam revocare constituit.
e) cum infans ceciderat, mater complexa eum in pedibus restituebat.
f) cum primum in proelium iniit, Caelius duo Gallos cecidit.
g) dummodo tibi placeat, hanc rationem instituam.
h) donec deos placaveritis, adversam fortunam patiemini.
i) dum omnes munus spectant, alter gladiator alterum gladio trucidavit.
j) vita fruere dum iuvenis eris!

Exercise 1B(i)

The theme of the Aeneid.

arma virumque cano, Troiae qui primus ab oris
Italiam fato profugus Lavinaque venit
Litora – multum ille et terris iactatus et alto
vi superum, saevae memorem Iunonis ob iram,
multa quoque et bello passus, **dum conderet** urbem
inferretque deos Latio – genus unde Latinum
Albanique patres atque altae moenia Romae.

Virgil, *Aeneid*

Exercise 1B(ii)

Neptune reassures Venus of his concern for Aeneas.

tum Saturnius haec domitor maris edidit alti:
'fas omne est, Cytherea, meis te fidere regnis,
unde genus ducis. merui quoque; saepe furores
compressi et rabiem tantam caelique marisque.
nec minor in terris, Xanthum Simoentaque testor,
Aeneae mihi cura tui. **cum** Troia Achilles
exanimata sequens **impingeret** agmina muris,
milia multa **daret** leto, **gemerent**que repleti
amnes nec reperire viam atque evolvere **posset**
in mare se Xanthus, Pelidae tunc ego forti
congressum Aenean nec dis nec viribus aequis
nube cava rapui, **cuperem cum** vertere ab imo
structa meis manibus periurae moenia Troiae.
nunc quoque mens eadem perstat mihi; pelle timores...'

Virgil, *Aeneid*

Exercise 1C

Arrius uses 'h's' inappropriately in his attempt to talk properly.

'chommoda' dicebat, si quando 'commoda' uellet[6]
dicere, et 'insidias' Arrius 'hinsidias',
et tum mirifice sperabat se[7] esse locutum,
cum quantum poterat **dixerat** 'hinsidias'.
credo, sic mater, sic liber auunculus eius,
sic maternus auus dixerat atque auia.
hoc misso in Syriam requierant omnibus aures;
audibant eadem haec leniter et leuiter,
nec sibi postilla metuebant talia uerba,
cum subito **affertur** nuntius horribilis,
Ionios fluctus[8], **postquam** illuc Arrius **isset**,
iam non Ionios esse sed Hionios.

Catullus

[6] See **9. Conditional Sentences C** ii) & **E** ii).
[7] See **2. Indirect Speech Part 2**.
[8] *Ionios fluctus...esse*: see **2. Indirect Speech Part 2**.

Exercises for Level Two

Exercise 2A

Death is non-existence.

[Seneca has recently suffered a bad attack of asthma...]

ego uero et in ipsa suffocatione non desii cogitationibus laetis ac fortibus acquiescere. 'quid hoc est?' inquam. 'tam saepe mors experitur me? faciat[9]: at ego illam diu expertus sum.' 'quando?' inquis. '**antequam nascerer**. mors est non esse. id quale sit[10] iam scio. hoc erit post me quod ante me fuit. si quid in hac re tormenti est, necesse est et fuisse[11], **antequam prodiremus** in lucem; atqui nullam sensimus tunc uexationem. rogo, non stultissimum dicas[12], si quis existimet lucernae peius esse[13] **cum extincta est** quam **antequam accenditur**? nos quoque et extinguimur et accendimur: medio illo tempore aliquid patimur; utrimque uero alta securitas est. in hoc enim, mi Lucili, nisi fallor, erramus, quod mortem[14] iudicamus sequi, **cum** illa et **praecesserit** et **secutura sit**. quicquid ante nos fuit, mors est. quid enim refert, non incipias[15] an desinas, **cum** utriusque rei hic **sit** effectus, non esse?'

Seneca, *Letters*

---

[9] *faciat*: see **8. Independent Subjunctives B** i).
[10] *id quale sit*: see **2. Indirect Speech Part 6**.
[11] *et fuisse*: 'that it existed also…'.
[12] *dicas, si...existimet*: see **9. Conditional Sentences C** i).
[13] *peius esse...*: see **2. Indirect Speech Part 2**.
[14] *mortem...sequi*: see **2. Indirect Speech Part 2**.
[15] *non incipias an...*: 'whether you do not begin or...'

Exercise 2B

Let us love until death do us part.

non ego laudari curo, mea Delia; tecum
  dum modo **sim**, quaeso, segnis inersque uocer.[16]
te spectem, suprema mihi **cum uenerit** hora;
  te teneam moriens deficiente manu.
flebis et arsuro positum me, Delia, lecto,
  tristibus et lacrimis oscula mixta dabis.
flebis: non tua sunt duro praecordia ferro
  uincta, nec in tenero stat tibi corde silex.
illo non iuuenis poterit de funere quisquam,
  lumina non uirgo sicca referre domum.
tu manes ne laede meos, sed parce solutis
  crinibus et teneris, Delia, parce genis.
interea, **dum** fata **sinunt**, iungamus[17] amores:
  iam ueniet tenebris Mors adoperta caput;[18]
iam subrepet iners aetas, neque amare decebit,
  dicere nec cano blanditias capite.
nunc leuis est tractanda[19] Venus, **dum** frangere postes
  non **pudet** et rixas inseruisse **iuuat**.
hic ego dux milesque bonus. uos, signa tubaeque,
  ite procul; cupidis uulnera ferte uiris,
ferte et opes: ego composito securus aceruo
  dites despiciam despiciamque famem.

Tibullus, *Elegies*

---

[16] *uocer...spectem...teneam*: see **8. Independent Subjunctives B** i).
[17] *iungamus*: see **8. Independent Subjunctives B** i).
[18] *caput*: an accusative of respect, for which see the **Glossary of Technical Terms**.
[19] *tractanda*: see **5. Gerunds and Gerundives D** a).

Exercise 2C

Come, Apollo, and attend your sacred rites.

Phoebe, faue: nouus ingreditur tua templa sacerdos:
huc, age, cum cithara carminibusque ueni.
nunc te uocales impellere pollice chordas,
nunc precor ad laudes flectere uerba mea.
ipse triumphali deuinctus tempora[20] lauro,
dum cumulant aras, ad tua sacra ueni.
sed nitidus pulcherque ueni: nunc indue uestem
sepositam, longas nunc bene pecte comas,
qualem te[21] memorant Saturno rege fugato
uictori laudes concinuisse Ioui.
tu procul euentura uides, tibi deditus augur
scit bene quid[22] fati prouida cantet auis;
tuque regis sortes, per te praesentit haruspex,
lubrica **signauit cum** deus exta notis;
te duce Romanos numquam frustrata[23] Sibylla,
abdita quae senis fata canit pedibus.[24]
Phoebe, sacras Messallinum sine tangere chartas
uatis, et ipse, precor, quid[25] canat illa doce.
haec dedit Aeneae sortes, **postquam** ille parentem
dicitur et raptos sustinuisse Lares;
nec fore[26] credebat Romam, **cum** maestus ab alto
Ilion ardentes **respiceret**que deos.

Tibullus, *Elegies*

---

[20] *tempora*: an accusative of respect, for which see the **Glossary of Technical Terms**.
[21] *te...concinuisse*: see **2. Indirect Speech Part 2**.
[22] *quid...cantet*: see **2. Indirect Speech Part 6**.
[23] *frustrata*: i.e. *frustrata est.*
[24] *senis...pedibus*: 'in six feet', i.e. in hexameters.
[25] *quid canat*: see **2. Indirect Speech Part 6**.
[26] *fore...Romam*: see **2. Indirect Speech Part 2**.

Exercises for Level Three

Exercises 3A & B

The fates of Camilla and Arruns.

A: *Arruns is granted part of his prayer and kills Camilla with an arrow.*

...et superos Arruns sic voce precatur:
'summe deum, sancti custos Soractis Apollo,
quem primi colimus, cui pineus ardor acervo
pascitur, et medium freti pietate per ignem
cultores multa premimus vestigia pruna,
da, pater, hoc nostris aboleri dedecus armis,
omnipotens. non exuvias pulsaeve tropaeum
virginis aut spolia ulla peto, mihi cetera laudem
facta ferent; haec dira meo **dum** vulnere pestis
pulsa **cadat**, patrias remeabo inglorius urbes.'
audiit et voti Phoebus succedere partem
mente dedit, partem volucris dispersit in auras:
sterneret ut[27] subita turbatam morte Camillam
adnuit oranti; reducem ut patria alta videret
non dedit, inque Notos vocem vertere procellae.
ergo **ut** missa manu sonitum **dedit** hasta per auras,
convertere animos acris oculosque tulere
cuncti ad reginam Volsci. nihil ipsa nec aurae
nec sonitus memor aut venientis ab aethere teli,
hasta sub exsertam **donec** perlata papillam
haesit virgineumque alte **bibit** acta cruorem.
concurrunt trepidae comites dominamque ruentem
suscipiunt.

Virgil, *Aeneid*

---

[27] *sterneret ut...ut...videret*: both clauses are dependent on *oranti*, 'to him praying that...'.

B: *Arruns meets the same fate at the hands of the goddess Opis.*

fugit ante omnis exterritus Arruns
laetitia mixtoque metu, nec iam amplius hastae
credere nec telis occurrere virginis audet.
ac velut ille, **prius quam** tela inimica **sequantur**,
continuo in montis sese avius abdidit altos
occiso pastore lupus magnove iuvenco,
conscius audacis facti, caudamque remulcens
subiecit pavitantem utero silvasque petivit:
haud secus ex oculis se turbidus abstulit Arruns
contentusque fuga mediis se immiscuit armis.
....
.... fuit ingens monte sub alto
regis Dercenni terreno ex aggere bustum
antiqui Laurentis opacaque ilice tectum;
hic dea[28] se primum rapido pulcherrima nisu
sistit et Arruntem tumulo speculatur ab alto.
ut vidit fulgentem armis ac vana tumentem,
'cur' inquit 'diversus abis? huc derige gressum,
huc periture veni, capias ut[29] digna Camillae
praemia. tune etiam telis moriere Dianae?'
dixit, et aurata volucrem Threissa sagittam
deprompsit pharetra cornuque infensa tetendit
et duxit longe, **donec** curvata **coirent**
inter se capita et manibus iam tangeret aequis,
laeva aciem ferri, dextra nervoque papillam.
extemplo teli stridorem aurasque sonantis
audiit una Arruns haesitque in corpore ferrum.
illum exspirantem socii atque extrema gementem
obliti ignoto camporum in pulvere linquunt;
Opis ad aetherium pennis aufertur Olympum.

Virgil, *Aeneid*

---

[28] *dea*: i.e. Opis.
[29] *ut*: see **6. Purpose and Result Clauses Part 1 B** i).

Exercises for Level Four

Exercise 4A

The sole survivor of the three Roman brothers, the Horatii, outwits the three Alban brothers, the Curiatii.

ad quorum casum **cum conclamasset** gaudio Albanus exercitus, Romanas legiones iam spes tota, nondum tamen cura deseruerat, exanimes uice unius quem tres Curiatii circumsteterant. forte is integer fuit, ut uniuersis solus nequaquam par, sic aduersus singulos ferox. ergo ut segregaret pugnam eorum capessit fugam, ita ratus secuturos ut quemque uolnere adfectum corpus sineret. iam aliquantum spatii ex eo loco **ubi pugnatum est** aufugerat, **cum** respiciens **uidet** magnis interuallis sequentes, unum haud procul ab sese abesse. in eum magno impetu rediit; et **dum** Albanus exercitus **inclamat** Curiatiis uti opem ferant fratri, iam Horatius caeso hoste uictor secundam pugnam petebat. tunc clamore qualis ex insperato fauentium solet Romani adiuuant militem suum; et ille defungi proelio festinat. **prius** itaque **quam** alter – nec procul aberat – consequi **posset**, et alterum Curiatium conficit; iamque aequato Marte singuli supererant, sed nec spe nec uiribus pares. alterum intactum ferro corpus et geminata uictoria ferocem in certamen tertium dabat: alter fessum uolnere, fessum cursu trahens corpus uictusque fratrum ante se strage uictori obicitur hosti. nec illud proelium fuit. Romanus exsultans 'duos' inquit, 'fratrum manibus dedi; tertium causae belli huiusce, ut Romanus Albano imperet, dabo.' male sustinenti arma gladium superne iugulo defigit, iacentem spoliat.

Livy

Exercise 4B

Ovid expresses undying gratitude to Rufus.

hoc tibi, Rufe, brevi properatum tempore mittit
Naso, parum faustae conditor Artis, opus,
ut, quamquam longe toto sumus orbe remoti,
scire tamen possis nos meminisse tui.
nominis **ante** mei venient oblivia nobis,
pectore **quam** pietas **sit** tua pulsa meo:
et **prius** hanc animam vacuas reddemus in auras,
quam fiat meriti gratia vana tui.
grande voco lacrimas meritum, quibus ora rigabas
cum mea concreto sicca dolore **forent**:
grande voco meritum maestae solacia mentis,
cum pariter nobis illa tibique **dares**.
sponte quidem per seque mea est laudabilis uxor,
admonitu melior fit tamen illa tuo.
namque quod Hermionae Castor fuit, Hector Iuli,
hoc ego te laetor coniugis esse meae.
quae ne dissimilis tibi sit probitate laborat,
seque tui vita sanguinis esse probat.
ergo quod fuerat stimulis factura sine ullis,
plenius auctorem te quoque nancta facit.
acer et ad palmae per se cursurus honores,
si tamen horteris, fortius ibit equus.
adde quod absentis cura mandata fideli
perficis, et nullum ferre gravaris onus.
o, referant grates, quoniam non possumus ipsi,
di tibi! qui referent, si pia facta vident;
sufficiatque diu corpus quoque moribus istis,
maxima Fundani gloria, Rufe, soli.

Ovid, *Epistulae ex Ponto*

Exercises for Level Five

Exercise 5A

Pompey's late wife, Julia, appears to him in a dream.

propulit ut classem uelis cedentibus Auster
incumbens mediumque rates mouere profundum,
omnis in Ionios spectabat nauita fluctus;
solus ab Hesperia non flexit lumina terra
Magnus, dum patrios portus, dum litora numquam
ad uisus reditura suos tectumque cacumen
nubibus et dubios cernit uanescere montis.
inde soporifero cesserunt languida somno
membra ducis; diri tum plena horroris imago
uisa caput maestum per hiantes Iulia terras
tollere et accenso furialis stare sepulchro.
'sedibus Elysiis campoque expulsa piorum
ad Stygias' inquit 'tenebras manesque nocentes
post bellum ciuile trahor; uidi ipsa tenentis
Eumenidas quaterent quas uestris lampadas armis;
praeparat innumeras puppis Acherontis adusti
portitor; in multas laxantur Tartara poenas;
uix operi cunctae dextra properante sorores
sufficiunt, lassant rumpentis stamina Parcas.
coniuge me laetos duxisti, Magne, triumphos:
fortuna est mutata toris, semperque potentis
detrahere in cladem fato damnata maritos
innupsit tepido paelex Cornelia busto.
haereat illa tuis per bella per aequora signis,
dum non securos liceat mihi rumpere somnos
et nullum uestro uacuum sit tempus amori,
sed teneat Caesarque dies et Iulia noctes.
me non Lethaeae, coniunx, obliuia ripae
inmemorem fecere tui, regesque silentum

permisere sequi. ueniam te bella gerente
in medias acies; numquam tibi, Magne, per umbras
perque meos manes genero non esse licebit.
abscidis frustra ferro tua pignora. bellum
te faciet ciuile meum.' sic fata refugit
umbra per amplexus trepidi dilapsa mariti.

Lucan, *De Bello Civili*

Exercise 5B

The origin of speech.

at varios linguae sonitus natura subegit
mittere et utilitas expressit nomina rerum,
non alia longe ratione atque ipsa videtur
protrahere ad gestum pueros infantia linguae,
cum facit ut digito quae sint praesentia monstrent.
sentit enim vis quisque suas quoad possit abuti.
cornua nata prius vitulo quam frontibus exstent,
illis iratus petit atque infestus inurget.
at catuli pantherarum scymnique leonum
unguibus ac pedibus iam tum morsuque repugnant,
vix etiam cum sunt dentes unguesque creati.
alituum porro genus alis omne videmus
fidere et a pinnis tremulum petere auxiliatum.
proinde putare aliquem tum nomina distribuisse
rebus et inde homines didicisse vocabula prima,
desiperest. nam cur hic posset cuncta notare
vocibus et varios sonitus emittere linguae,
tempore eodem alii facere id non quisse putentur?
praeterea si non alii quoque vocibus usi
inter se fuerant, unde insita notities est
utilitatis et unde data est huic prima potestas,
quid vellet facere ut sciret animoque videret?
cogere item pluris unus victosque domare
non poterat, rerum ut perdiscere nomina vellent.

nec ratione docere ulla suadereque surdis,
quid sit opus facto, facilest; neque enim paterentur
nec ratione ulla sibi ferrent amplius auris
vocis inauditos sonitus obtundere frustra.
postremo quid in hac mirabile tantoperest re,
si genus humanum, cui vox et lingua vigeret,
pro vario sensu varia res voce notaret?
cum pecudes mutae, cum denique saecla ferarum
dissimilis soleant voces variasque ciere,
cum metus aut dolor est et cum iam gaudia gliscunt.
quippe etenim licet id rebus cognoscere apertis.
irritata canum cum primum magna Molossum
mollia ricta fremunt duros nudantia dentis,
longe alio sonitu rabie restricta minantur,
et cum iam latrant et vocibus omnia complent.

Lucretius, *De Rerum Natura*

Chapter 5

GERUNDS AND GERUNDIVES

Parallel Revision: Forms of Gerunds & Gerundives, Kennedy 116-25, 137, CLG 7f.12-13, OLG pp. 37-56, 59-61, 108.

A. What are Gerunds and Gerundives?

i) **Gerunds**. All verbs, e.g. 'learn', 'understand', 'be', denote actions or states. Behind these actions or states lie *concepts*, usually expressed in English by the addition of '-ing', here 'learning', 'understanding' and 'being' respectively. In the context of the following sentences

> 'Men do not become wise by the *learning* of facts alone.'
>
> 'An *understanding* of grammar is a useful, transferable skill.'

it is clear that '(the) learning' and '(an) understanding' are nouns. They are in fact **gerunds**. So, gerunds are **verbal nouns** and in Latin are always **active** in sense.

ii) **Gerundives**, on the other hand, are **verbal adjectives** and **passive** in sense. As adjectives, gerundives are a form of the verb which describes nouns. In the English language we have no single word equivalent to the Latin gerundive. A literal translation of a gerundive is in fact completely alien to our own way of speaking, e.g. '(the art of letters)-*being-written*', where the gerundive-phrase 'being-written' is passive and describes the noun 'letters'. Since English favours the active over the passive voice, after translating a gerundive literally, as shown, it is sensible to turn the phrase around, giving the more fluent '(the art of) *letter-writing*'.

B. How do we distinguish a gerund from a gerundive in a text?

i) **Gerunds** occur only in **singular** forms. These forms are **neuter** in gender and of the second declension type. Gerunds can, therefore, only end in *-um, -i, -o*.

ii) **Gerundives** are adjectives and can qualify nouns of any gender and number (i.e. masculine, feminine or neuter, and singular or plural). They therefore occur in **any ending** of the **first/second declension adjective** type, i.e. *-us, -a, -um* etc.

iii) Since gerundives are adjectives, whose function is to describe nouns, the **noun** described by the gerundive will normally also be **expressed** in the immediate context and will be recognizable by having the **same case, number and gender**, e.g. *usus in oratione habenda* 'experience (lit. in a speech-being-delivered) in delivering a speech'.

iv) A verb which is intransitive (see **Glossary of Technical Terms**) occurs in the passive only in an impersonal construction (e.g. *ventum est*, lit. 'it was come', *ei persuadetur*, lit. 'it is persuaded to him'). Similarly, **intransitive verbs** occur as **gerundives only** in an **impersonal** sense in the **nominative** case [see below **D** a)]. In all other cases **intransitive verbs** only have **gerund** forms.

v) The Romans preferred gerundives to gerunds. So, instead of saying 'the art of *waging* wars', where 'waging' is an active verbal noun governing a direct object, they preferred to say 'the art of wars-*being waged*', where 'being waged' is an adjectival phrase describing the noun 'wars'. **Gerundives,** therefore, are **more common** than gerunds.

C. Coping with Gerunds and Gerundives: the first step

A common misconception concerning gerunds and gerundives is that a translation appropriate to one found in the nominative can be applied to one used in another case or vice versa. However, Latin used gerunds and gerundives in ways **specific to each case**.[1] So establish the case of a gerund or gerundive *first* and then use the advice given below regarding an appropriate translation.

D. Gerunds and Gerundives: the different cases[2]

a) **Nominative (gerundives only[3])**: in the nominative case, gerundives are found with some form of the verb *sum* **'I am'** and express **obligation**, i.e. they indicate that something '*must* be done'.[4] The person who must do something (i.e. the agent of the action) is usually expressed by the **dative** case. The following formulae may be applied to most gerundives as a means of establishing a literal translation:

---

[1] There are a few words which in form and origin are gerundives, but which came to be used largely as ordinary adjectives, e.g. *horrendus*, *invidendus*, *tremendus*, *nefandus*, *infandus* etc. The rules governing the specific usage of gerunds and gerundives do not apply to words of this type, which are usually distinguished from 'true' gerunds and gerundives by their own separate entry in dictionaries.

[2] Since, as indicated above, there is nothing in the English language akin to the 'gerundive' turn of phrase, the following descriptions of specific uses of gerunds and gerundives mostly show the literal translation of the gerundive in brackets, merely as a guide to establishing the sense of the phrase.

[3] The gerund does not occur in the nominative.

[4] Various English words derived from gerundives still show this sense of obligation: Amanda-a girl who 'must be loved', Miranda-a girl who 'must be admired', referendum-a matter which 'must be referred', agendum/agenda-a matter/ matters which 'must be done', addendum-something which 'must be added'. The abbreviation Q.E.D. also conceals a gerundive, *quod erat demonstrandum*-a matter 'which one was required to demonstrate'; it has therefore traditionally been appended to a student's final answer to mathematical problems.

Tense of *sum*	**English formulae for translating gerundive**
Present	'x (nom.) **must be done** by y (dat.)'
Future	'x (nom.) **will have to be done** by y (dat.)'
Past	'x (nom.) **should have been done** by y (dat.)'

Having established this literal translation, you may prefer to turn the sentence around to avoid using the passive verb. So:

nemini Vestales stuprandae sunt. **(present)**
'The Vestal Virgins must be defiled by no-one.'/
'No-one must defile the Vestal Virgins.'

exercitui flumen transeundum erit. **(future)**
'The river will have to be crossed by the army.'/
'The army will have to cross the river.'

hostibus obsides iam tradendi erant. **(imperfect)**
'The hostages should already have been handed over by the enemy.'/
'The enemy should already have handed over the hostages.'

It is not possible, however, to apply these formulae to **nominative gerundives of intransitive verbs** or verbs used intransitively, for which use instead:

Tense of *sum*	**Formulae for intransitive gerundives**
Present	'It **is necessary** for x (dat.) to…' OR 'x (dat.) **must**…'
Future	'It **will be necessary** for x (dat.) to…' OR 'x (dat.) **will have to**…'
Past	'It **was necessary** for x (dat.) to…' OR 'x (dat.) **should have**…'

So:

ante noctem vobis perveniendum est. **(present)**
'It is necessary for you to arrive before nightfall.'/
'You must arrive before nightfall.'
pueris laborandum erit. **(future)**
'It will be necessary for the boys to work hard.'/
'The boys will have to work hard.'
senatoribus haudquaquam in rempublicam conspirandum erat. **(perfect)**
'Senators should by no means have conspired against the state.'

In certain circumstances, the use of the **dative** to show the agent of a gerundive may lead to confusion. This may occur, for example, where the speaker wishes to use a second dative to express an indirect object of the verb. If in this context a dative is also used to express the agent of the action, e.g.,

nobis Romanis resistendum est.

it is impossible to distinguish the dative of agent from the dative of the indirect object. Should we translate the above as

'It is necessary for us to resist the Romans.'/
'We must resist the Romans.'

or as

'It is necessary for the Romans to resist us.'/
'The Romans must resist us.'?

Latin avoids the ambiguity inherent in this situation by replacing the dative of agent with *a/ab* + the ablative case:

a nobis Romanis resistendum est.

clearly means

'It is necessary for us to resist the Romans.'/
'We must resist the Romans'.

b) The **accusative** of gerunds and gerundives occurs in five main contexts:

i) (gerundive only) in **indirect statements**, expressing obligation in place of the nominative gerundive, since the subject in an indirect statement is indicated by the accusative and not the nominative. The accusative of a gerundive expressing obligation within an indirect statement follows the same rules as those given for the nominative case above:

> *imperator militibus dixit proelium imminere; eis audendum pugnandumque pro virili parte esse.*
> 'The general told his soldiers that the battle was imminent; that it was necessary for them to be bold and to fight to the best of their ability.'

ii) in phrases composed of **adjectives + *ad***, e.g. *paratus ad* 'prepared for *do*ing/(x being *done*)':

> *angustiae aptae ad insidias comparandas sunt.*
> 'Narrow defiles are suitable for laying ambushes.'

iii) after the prepositions ***ad*** or ***ob*** to indicate **purpose**, lit. 'for the purpose of *do*ing/(x being *done*)':

> *victi ob mortem certam vitandam fugiebant.*
> 'The defeated men fled in order to avoid certain death.'

iv) (gerundive only) in the phrase **curo x (acc.) + gerundive, 'I see to x being *done*'**:

> *praefectus commeatus portandos curabat.*
> 'The captain saw (lit. to the provisions being transported) to the transportation of the provisions.'

v) (gerundive only) in agreement with the direct object of a verb in the sense **'to be *done*'**:

> *filius Lari aurum servandum dedit.*
> 'The son gave his gold to the Lar to be looked after.'

c) The **genitive** of gerunds and gerundives is found:
i) with nouns and adjectives that regularly take the genitive; translate '**of doing**/(x being *done*)':

> *Ratio bene dicendi a multis docetur, a paucis discitur.*
> 'The art of speaking well is taught by many, learnt by few.'

ii) with the ablative of ***causa*** and ***gratia*** to express '**for the sake of doing**/(x being *done*)', '**in order to**...':

> *multi honoris gradus gloriae sibi consequendae gratia petunt.*
> 'Many seek the ranks of office in order to win glory for themselves.'

d) The **dative** of gerunds and gerundives occurs with verbs and phrases which regularly take a dative. Translate '**to doing**/(x being *done*)' or '**for doing**/(x being *done*)'.

> *multi bene vivendo, pauci bene moriendo operam dant.*
> 'Many pay attention to living well, few to dying well.'

e) The **ablative** of gerunds and gerundives:
i) usually expresses **instrument**, i.e. '**by doing**/(x being *done*)':

> *tiro fortis fiet perferendis laboribus.*
> 'The young soldier will become strong by patiently enduring hardships.'

ii) also occurs after certain **prepositions** requiring the ablative, primarily ***in*** and ***de***:

> *tempus in fabulis audiendis tritum est.*
> 'Time was wasted in listening to stories.'

Exercises for Level One

Exercise 1A

The gerunds & gerundives below follow the same order as the descriptions given above of their various uses in different cases. For each sentence establish first whether you have a gerund or gerundive and then translate.

a) tibi aes alienum persolvendum erit.
b) philosophi opinantur animos ad altiora advertendos esse.
c) tubicen semper paratus ad signum proelii dandum est.
d) ambo duces in medium progressi sunt ob condiciones pacis disserendas.
e) Caesar pontem reficiendum curavit.
f) eis multam praedam inter ipsos distribuendam dedit.
g) Ulixes consilium Troiae penetrandae capiebat.
h) Medea suos prodiderat Iasoni subveniendi causa.
i) clientes operam patronis salutandis dant.
j) Catilina animis civium excitandis res novare constituit.

Exercise 1B[V]

The gerunds & gerundives appear in this exercise in random order. Establish first what case each gerund or gerundive is in and then follow the guidelines given above for translation.

a) Flavia in filio pariendo mortua est.
b) dominus multos coquos ad nuptias parandas conducebat.
c) ab omnibus parendum legibus est.
d) omnibus pari iure cum civibus vivendum est.
e) ille humanissimus oppidum mulieribus liberisque parcendi causa haud incendit.
f) amico placendi causa testis multum periurabat.
g) dis placandis multam operam dabat consul.
h) docendo permulta discimus.
i) rebus adversis militibus audendum est.
j) oratio unius cuiusque oratoris iudicibus audienda est.

Exercise 1C

Moderation is golden when navigating through the sea of life.

rectius vives, Licini, neque altum
semper **urgendo** neque, dum procellas
cautus horrescis, nimium **premendo**
litus iniquum.

auream quisquis mediocritatem
diligit, tutus caret obsoleti
sordibus tecti, caret invidenda[5]
sobrius aula.

Horace, *Odes*

Exercise 1D

A philosopher who does not practise what he preaches is as useless as a sea-sick helmsman.

nullos[6] autem peius mereri de omnibus mortalibus iudico quam qui philosophiam uelut aliquod artificium uenale didicerunt, qui aliter uiuunt quam **uiuendum** esse[7] praecipiunt. exempla enim se ipsos inutilis disciplinae circumferunt, nulli non uitio, quod insequuntur, obnoxii. non magis mihi potest quisquam talis prodesse praeceptor quam gubernator in tempestate nauseabundus. **tenendum** rapiente fluctu gubernaculum, **luctandum** cum ipso mari, **eripienda** sunt uento uela: quid me potest adiuuare rector nauigii attonitus et uomitans? quanto maiore[8] putas uitam[9] tempestate iactari quam ullam ratem? non est **loquendum**, sed **gubernandum**.

Seneca, *Letters*

---

[5] *invidenda*: see note 1 above.
[6] *nullos...mereri*: see **2. Indirect Speech Part 2**.
[7] *uiuendum esse*: see **2. Indirect Speech Part 2**.
[8] *quanto maiore*: 'how much more...?'.
[9] *uitam...iactari*: see **2. Indirect Speech Part 2**.

Exercises for Level Two

Exercise 2A

a) arte citae veloque rates remoque moventur,
arte leves currus: arte regendus Amor. (Ovid)

b) quanto satius est quid faciendum sit quam quid factum quaerere! (Seneca)

c) desine fata deum flecti sperare precando. (Virgil)

d) vota aliis facienda deis. (Valerius Flaccus)

e) et mihi discendi et tibi docendi facultatem otium praebet. (Pliny)

f) audendum est: fortes adiuuat ipsa Venus. (Tibullus)

g) stulta est enim, mi Lucili, et minime conveniens litterato viro occupatio exercendi lacertos et dilatandi cervicem ac latera firmandi. (Seneca)

h) Caesar dando sublevando ignoscundo, Cato nihil largiundo gloriam adeptus est. (Sallust)

i) desperanda tibi salva concordia socru. (Juvenal)

j) videbaturque Nero condendae urbis novae et cognomento suo appellandae gloriam quaerere. (Tacitus)

Exercise 2B

Much is at stake in this war.

causa quae sit[10] videtis: nunc quid **agendum** sit considerate. primum mihi videtur de genere belli, deinde de magnitudine, tum de imperatore **deligendo** esse **dicendum**. genus est belli eiusmodi, quod maxime vestros animos excitare atque inflammare ad **persequendi** studium debeat[11]: in quo agitur populi Romani gloria, quae vobis a maioribus cum[12] magna in omnibus rebus, tum summa in re militari tradita est; agitur salus sociorum atque amicorum, pro qua multa maiores vestri magna et gravia bella gesserunt; aguntur certissima populi Romani vectigalia et maxima, quibus amissis et pacis ornamenta et subsidia belli requiretis; aguntur bona multorum civium, quibus est a vobis et ipsorum et rei publicae causa **consulendum**.

Cicero, *De Imperio*

Exercise 2C

Dido rebukes Aeneas for abandoning her and Carthage.

certus es ire tamen miseramque relinquere Didon,
    atque idem venti vela fidemque ferent?
certus es, Aenea, cum foedere solvere naves,
    quaeque ubi sint[13] nescis, Itala regna sequi?
nec nova Carthago, nec te crescentia tangunt
    moenia nec sceptro tradita summa tuo?
facta[14] fugis, **facienda** petis; **quaerenda** per orbem
    altera, quaesita est altera terra tibi.
ut[15] terram invenias, quis eam tibi tradet **habendam**?
    quis sua non notis arva **tenenda** dabit?

Ovid, *Heroides*

---

[10] *quae sit...quid agendum sit...*: see **2. Indirect Speech Part 6**.
[11] *debeat*: see **6. Purpose and Result Clauses Part 2 B**.
[12] *cum...tum*: see **4. Temporal Conjunctions E** vii).
[13] *ubi sint*: see **2. Indirect Speech Part 6**.
[14] *facta...facienda*: i.e. *ea quae facta sunt...ea quae facienda sunt*.
[15] *ut...invenias*: 'though you may find...'.

Exercises for Level Three

Exercise 3A

Let each man be content with the length of his life.

quod cuique temporis ad **vivendum** datur, eo debet esse contentus. neque enim histrioni, ut[16] placeat, **peragenda** fabula est, modo in quocumque fuerit actu probetur, neque sapienti usque ad 'plaudite'[17] **veniendum** est. breve enim tempus aetatis satis longum est ad bene honesteque **vivendum**; sin processerit longius, non magis **dolendum** est, quam agricolae dolent praeterita verni temporis suavitate aestatem autumnumque venisse. ver enim tamquam adulescentiam significat ostenditque fructus futuros, reliqua autem tempora **demetendis** fructibus et **percipiendis** accommodata sunt. fructus autem senectutis est, ut saepe dixi, ante partorum bonorum memoria et copia. omnia autem, quae secundum naturam fiunt, sunt **habenda** in bonis.

Cicero, *De Senectute*

---

[16] *ut placeat*: see **6. Purpose and Result Clauses Part 1 B** i).

[17] *'plaudite'*: 'Applause, please!', as addressed to the audience at the end of a play.

Exercise 3B

Much labour is involved in caring for vines.[18]

est etiam ille labor **curandis** vitibus alter,
cui numquam exhausti satis est: namque omne quotannis
terque quaterque solum **scindendum** glaebaque versis
aeternum **frangenda** bidentibus, omne **levandum**
fronde nemus. redit agricolis labor actus in orbem,
atque in se sua per vestigia volvitur annus.
ac iam olim, seras posuit cum vinea frondes
frigidus et silvis Aquilo decussit honorem,
iam tum acer curas venientem extendit in annum
rusticus, et curvo Saturni dente relictam
persequitur vitem attondens fingitque **putando**.
primus humum fodito, primus devecta cremato
sarmenta, et vallos primus sub tecta referto;
postremus metito. bis vitibus ingruit umbra,
bis segetem densis obducunt sentibus herbae;
durus uterque labor: laudato ingentia rura,
exiguum colito. nec non etiam aspera rusci
vimina per silvam et ripis fluvialis harundo
caeditur, incultique exercet cura salicti.
iam vinctae vites, iam falcem arbusta reponunt,
iam canit effectos extremus vinitor antes:
sollicitanda tamen tellus pulvisque **movendus**,
et iam maturis **metuendus** Iuppiter uvis.

Virgil, *Georgics*

[18] Given the specialised nature of the vocabulary in this passage, allow yourself to look up *puto, sarmentum, sentis, ruscum, salictum, arbustus, antes* before attempting to translate.

Exercises for Level Four

Exercise 4A

It is necessary to harden the mind.

id agere debemus ut irritamenta uitiorum quam longissime profugiamus. **indurandus** est animus et a blandimentis uoluptatum procul **abstrahendus**. una Hannibalem hiberna soluerunt et indomitum illum niuibus atque Alpibus uirum eneruauerunt fomenta Campaniae. armis uicit, uitiis uictus est. nobis quoque **militandum** est, et quidem genere militiae quo numquam quies, numquam otium datur. **debellandae** sunt imprimis uoluptates, quae, ut uides, saeua quoque ad se ingenia rapuerunt. si quis sibi proposuerit quantum operis aggressus sit, sciet nihil delicate, nihil molliter esse **faciendum**. quid mihi cum istis calentibus stagnis? quid cum sudatoriis, in quae siccus uapor corpora exhausturus includitur? omnis sudor per laborem exeat. si faceremus quod fecit Hannibal, ut interrupto cursu rerum omissoque bello **fouendis** corporibus operam daremus, nemo non intempestiuam desidiam, uictori quoque, nedum uincenti, periculosam, merito reprenderet: minus nobis quam illis Punica signa sequentibus licet, plus periculi restat cedentibus, plus operis etiam perseuerantibus. fortuna mecum bellum gerit: non sum imperata facturus. iugum non recipio, immo, quod maiore uirtute **faciendum** est, excutio. non est **emolliendus** animus: si uoluptati cessero, **cedendum** est dolori, **cedendum** est labori, **cedendum** est paupertati.

Seneca, *Letters*

Exercise 4B

Cicero explains why he has never before spoken on the rostra.

quamquam mihi semper frequens conspectus vester multo iucundissimus, hic autem locus ad **agendum** amplissimus, ad **dicendum** ornatissimus est visus, Quirites, tamen hoc aditu laudis, qui semper optimo cuique maxime patuit, non mea me voluntas adhuc, sed vitae meae rationes ab ineunte aetate susceptae prohibuerunt: nam cum antea per aetatem nondum huius auctoritatem loci attingere auderem statueremque nihil huc nisi perfectum ingenio, elaboratum industria adferri oportere, omne meum tempus amicorum temporibus **transmittendum** putavi. ita neque hic locus vacuus umquam fuit ab eis, qui vestram causam defenderent, et meus labor in privatorum periculis caste integreque versatus ex vestro iudicio fructum est amplissimum consecutus. nam cum propter dilationem comitiorum ter praetor primus centuriis cunctis renuntiatus sum, facile intellexi, Quirites, et quid de me iudicaretis et quid aliis praescriberetis. nunc, cum et auctoritatis in me tantum sit, quantum vos honoribus **mandandis** esse voluistis, et ad **agendum** facultatis tantum, quantum homini viliganti ex forensi usu prope cotidiana **dicendi** exercitatio potuit adferre, certe et si quid auctoritatis in me est, apud eos utar, qui eam mihi dederunt, et si quid in **dicendo** consequi possum, eis ostendam potissimum, qui ei quoque rei fructum suo iudicio **tribuendum** esse duxerunt. atque illud in primis mihi **laetandum** iure esse video, quod in hac insolita mihi ex hoc loco ratione **dicendi** causa talis oblata est, in qua oratio deesse nemini possit: **dicendum** est enim de Cn. Pompeii singulari eximiaque virtute; huius autem orationis difficilius est exitum quam principium invenire; ita mihi non tam copia quam modus in **dicendo** **quaerendus** est.

Cicero, *De Imperio*

Exercise 4C

Medea begs Creon for one last wish before she must depart in exile.

MEDEA

profugere cogis? redde fugienti ratem
vel redde comitem-fugere cur solam iubes?
non sola veni. bella si metuis pati,
utrumque regno pelle. cur sontes duos
distinguis? illi Pelia[19], non nobis iacet;
fugam, rapinas adice, desertum patrem
lacerumque fratrem, quidquid etiam nunc novas
docet maritus coniuges, non est meum:
totiens nocens sum facta, sed numquam mihi.

CREO

iam exisse decuit. quid seris **fando** moras?

MEDEA

supplex recedens illud extremum precor,
ne culpa natos matris insontes trahat.

CREO

vade: hos paterno ut genitor excipiam sinu.

MEDEA

per ego auspicatos regii thalami toros,
per spes futuras perque regnorum status,
Fortuna varia dubia quos agitat vice,
precor, brevem largire fugienti moram,
dum extrema natis mater infigo oscula,
fortasse moriens.

CREO

fraudibus tempus petis.

MEDEA

quae fraus timeri tempore exiguo potest?

CREO

nullum ad **nocendum** tempus angustum est malis.

---

[19] *Pelia* is nominative here.

MEDEA
parumne miserae temporis lacrimis negas?
CREO
etsi repugnat precibus infixus timor,
unus **parando** dabitur exilio dies.
MEDEA
nimis est, recidas aliquid ex isto licet:
et ipsa propero.
CREO
capite supplicium lues,
clarum priusquam Phoebus attollat diem
nisi cedis Isthmo. sacra me thalami vocant,
vocat precari festus Hymenaeo dies.

Seneca, *Medea*

Exercises for Level Five

Exercise 5A

Quintilian suggests good practice in teaching.

his fere, quae in proximos quinque libros collata sunt, ratio inveniendi atque inventa disponendi continetur, quam ut per omnes numeros penitus cognoscere ad summam scientiae necessarium est, ita incipientibus brevius ac simplicius tradi magis convenit. aut enim difficultate institutionis tam numerosae atque perplexae deterreri solent, aut eo tempore, quo praecipue alenda ingenia atque indulgentia quadam enutrienda sunt, asperiorum tractatu rerum atteruntur, aut, si haec sola didicerunt, satis se ad eloquentiam instructos arbitrantur, aut quasi ad certas quasdam dicendi leges adligati conatum omnem reformidant. unde existimant accidisse ut, qui diligentissimi artium scriptores exstiterint, ab eloquentia longissime fuerint. via tamen opus est incipientibus, sed ea plana et cum ad ingrediendum tum ad demonstrandum expedita. eligat itaque peritus ille praeceptor ex omnibus optima et tradat ea demum in praesentia quae placet, remota refutandi cetera mora. sequentur enim discipuli, quo duxeris. mox cum robore dicendi crescet etiam eruditio. iidem primo solum iter credant esse in quod inducentur, mox illud cognituri etiam optimum. sunt autem neque obscura neque ad percipiendum difficilia quae scriptores diversis opinionibus pertinaciter tuendis involverunt. itaque in toto artis huiusce tractatu difficilius est iudicare quid doceas quam, cum iudicaris, docere, praecipueque in duabus his partibus perquam sunt pauca, circa quae si is qui instituitur non repugnaverit, pronum ad cetera habiturus est cursum.

Quintilian, *Institutio Oratoria*

Exercise 5B

Pliny opens his panegyric on Trajan.

bene ac sapienter, patres conscripti, maiores instituerunt ut rerum agendarum ita dicendi initium a precationibus capere, quod nihil rite nihil providenter homines sine deorum immortalium ope consilio honore auspicarentur. qui mos cui potius quam consuli aut quando magis usurpandus colendusque est, quam cum imperio senatus, auctoritate rei publicae ad agendas optimo principi gratias excitamur? quod enim praestabilius est aut pulchrius munus deorum, quam castus et sanctus et dis simillimus princeps? ac si adhuc dubium fuisset, forte casuque rectores terris an aliquo numine darentur, principem tamen nostrum liqueret divinitus constitutum. non enim occulta potestate fatorum, sed ab Iove ipso coram ac palam repertus electus est: quippe inter aras et altaria, eodemque loci quem deus ille tam manifestus ac praesens quam caelum ac sidera insedit. quo magis aptum piumque est te, Iuppiter optime, antea conditorem, nunc conservatorem imperii nostri precari, ut mihi digna consule digna senatu digna principe contingat oratio, utque omnibus quae dicentur a me, libertas fides veritas constet, tantumque a specie adulationis absit gratiarum actio mea quantum abest a necessitate. equidem non consuli modo sed omnibus civibus enitendum reor, ne quid de principe nostro ita dicant, ut idem illud de alio dici potuisse videatur. quare abeant ac recedant voces illae quas metus exprimebat. nihil quale ante dicamus, nihil enim quale antea patimur; nec eadem de principe palam quae prius praedicemus, neque enim eadem secreto quae prius loquimur. discernatur orationibus nostris diversitas temporum, et ex ipso genere gratiarum agendarum intellegatur, cui quando sint actae. nusquam ut deo, nusquam ut numini blandiamur: non enim de tyranno sed de cive, non de domino sed de parente loquimur.

Pliny, *Panegyricus*

Exercise 5C

Measures to combat trickery.

postquam ab eo conloquio in arcem sese recepit, conuocatis militibus ‘credo ego uos audisse, milites’ inquit, ‘quemadmodum praesidia Romana ab Siculis circumuenta et oppressa sint per hos dies. eam uos fraudem deum primo benignitate, dein uestra ipsi uirtute dies noctesque perstando ac peruigilando in armis uitastis. utinam reliquum tempus nec patiendo infanda nec faciendo traduci possit. haec occulta in fraude cautio est qua usi adhuc sumus; cui quoniam parum succedit, aperte ac propalam claues portarum reposcunt; quas simul tradiderimus, Carthaginiensium extemplo Henna erit foediusque hic trucidabimur quam Murgantiae praesidium interfectum est. noctem unam aegre ad consultandum sumpsi, qua uos certiores periculi instantis facerem. orta luce contionem habituri sunt ad criminandum me concitandumque in uos populum. itaque crastino die aut uestro aut Hennensium sanguine Henna inundabitur. nec praeoccupati spem ullam nec occupantes periculi quicquam habebitis; qui prior strinxerit ferrum, eius uictoria erit. intenti ergo omnes armatique signum exspectabitis. ego in contione ero et tempus, quoad omnia instructa sint, loquendo altercandoque traham. cum toga signum dedero, tum mihi undique clamore sublato turbam inuadite ac sternite omnia ferro; et cauete quisquam supersit cuius aut uis aut fraus timeri possit. uos, Ceres mater ac Proserpina, precor, ceteri superi infernique di, qui hanc urbem, hos sacratos lacus lucosque colitis, ut ita nobis uolentes propitii adsitis, si uitandae, non inferendae fraudis causa hoc consilii capimus.’

Livy

Chapter 6
PURPOSE AND RESULT CLAUSES

Parallel Revision: Perfect, Pluperfect and Future Perfect Indicatives of Active, Passive, Deponent and Irregular Verbs, Kennedy 115-25, 133-9, *CLG* 7b-c, 8a, 9.1, *OLG* pp. 36-60.

Part 1. Purpose Clauses

A. What are Purpose Clauses?

Purpose clauses are subordinate clauses showing the intention or purpose of an action:

> 'I wrote this letter *in order that you might understand my point of view.*'
>
> 'The soldiers turned tail *in order to break the ranks of the enemy.*'
>
> 'A messenger came *to announce the army's victory to the senate and the Roman people.*'

As these examples demonstrate, English introduces purpose clauses by using **'in order that'**, **'in order to'** or simply **'to'**.

Latin constructs purpose clauses in three main ways. In each case, the verb of the purpose clause is in the **subjunctive**.

B. *ut/ne* + subjunctive:

i) *ut/ne* with the subjunctive is by far the most common type of purpose clause found in Latin. *ut* introduces purpose clauses which contain no form of negative (such as 'not', 'nothing', 'no-one' etc.). Where such a negative does belong within the purpose clause, it is expressed by *ne*, which replaces *ut*. After *ne*, *quis*/*quid* etc. means 'anyone/anything' etc.

Cicero Baias iit ut otio frueretur.
'Cicero went to Baiae to enjoy some free time.'
mentiebar ne quis te reprehenderet.
'I lied in order that no-one would blame you.'

Certain words and phrases sometimes act as a 'signpost' that a purpose clause is imminent. These words include:

eo, ideo, propterea, ad hoc, ob eam rem etc.

all meaning 'for this reason/purpose':[1]

haec eo dico ut res gravissimas intellegatis.
'I say these things for this reason, (in order) that you may understand these very serious matters.'

ii) In a few instances, instead of indicating the purpose of an action itself, purpose clauses introduced by *ut* refer allusively to the writer's purpose in *mentioning* a matter:

<u>ut</u> illa omittam, <u>ut</u> fulminum iactus, <u>ut</u> terrae motus relinquam, <u>ut</u> omittam cetera, hoc certe neque praetermittendum neque relinquendum est. (Cicero)
'To omit those things, to pass over thunderbolts, to leave aside earthquakes, to omit all the rest, this certainly must be neither passed over nor left aside.'

The multiple phrases introduced by *ut* in this sentence suggest Cicero's purpose in describing *hoc*, 'this', in detail: by indicating his intention to pass over in a single word certain topics (*illa*) which are normally worthy of greater mention, Cicero stamps on his audience an immediate impression of how much more significant 'this' is. Purpose clauses of this nature are best translated into English by the infinitive, '**to...**'.

---

[1] It is particularly important to observe the use of *eo* (ablative of *is*, *ea*, *id*) in this sense, as this word is so easily confused with *eo*, 'I go'. *eo* in this sense is also a common precursor to *quod* with the indicative, 'for this reason...because'.

C. In place of *ut/ne*, the relative pronoun ***qui, quae, quod*** can also introduce a purpose clause, especially after a verb in the main clause indicating or implying motion. This purpose clause is distinguished from ordinary, purely adjectival relative clauses[2] by the use of a **subjunctive** verb. The relative pronoun may be retained in translation, the notion of purpose being indicated by the phrase '**who/which was to**' or '**who/which were to**', etc.

> *praetor consuli litteras complures mittebat quae eum novae seditionis admonerent.*
> 'The praetor sent the consul several letters which were to warn him of a new uprising.'

D. *quo* is used in place of *ut*, where a **comparative adjective** or **adverb** occurs in a purpose clause:

> *eadem identidem explicabat quo melius intellegerent.*
> 'He explained the same things over and over again in order that they might understand them better.'

This usage of *quo* can be distinguished from others[3] by the presence of the comparative adjective/adverb *and* the subjunctive verb.

---

[2] For which see **1. Relative Clauses.**

[3] See **10. Coping with *qui* E** c).

Part 2. Result Clauses

There are two main types of result clause in Latin. In each case, the verb of the result clause is in the **subjunctive**.

A. As the name suggests, the most common type of result clause is a subordinate clause showing the consequence or **result** of the action or situation expressed in the main clause:

> 'He was so powerful *that he could strangle an ox with his bare hands.*'
>
> 'They brought so much food *that we could not eat it all*'.
>
> 'The orator spoke in such a way *that we were all moved to pity.*'

The clause governing the result clause usually contains a word or phrase which indicates *why* the result expressed was inevitable: in the above sentences these words are 'so (powerful)', 'so much (food)' and 'in such a way', respectively. Words and phrases of this nature in Latin include:

Latin	English
tam + adjective or adverb	'so x (adj. or adv.) (that)…'
talis, -e	'of such a kind (that)…'
tantus, -a, -um	'so great (that)…'
totiens	'so many times (that)…'
tot	'so many (that)…'
adeo	'to such an extent (that)…'
eo + genitive	'to such a point of x (that)…'
ita/sic	'in such a way (that)…'

Result clauses of this nature are introduced by ***ut***, with *non/ numquam/nusquam* etc. added as appropriate where a negative is required.[4] The verb is in the **subjunctive**:

> *Achilles tam fortis erat ut nemo eibi resistere posset.*
> 'Achilles was so strong that no-one could withstand him.'
> *puer patrem canem totiens poscebat ut eum tandem acciperet.*
> 'The boy asked his father for a dog so many times that at last he received one.'

B. The second type of result clause is introduced by the relative pronoun, ***qui, quae, quod***. In result clauses of this type, the result or consequence expressed depends not on an *action* or *situation* in the governing clause but on a **characteristic of the antecedent**; that is to say, the antecedent does not *do* anything to produce the result expressed in the result clause: this result is a consequence of what the antecedent is *by its very nature*. Since these result clauses indicate a characteristic of the antecedent in this way, they are sometimes referred to as 'generic' results, from the Latin *genus, generis* 'kind/type', and the verb in the clause is often called a 'generic subjunctive'. 'Generic' result clauses tend to occur in the following contexts:

i) after certain pronouns, most notably ***is ea id***:

> *orator bonus ea dicit quae auditores benevolos attentos faciles faciant.*
> 'A good orator says (the sort of) things which make listeners well-disposed, attentive and compliant.'

---

[4] NB: *ne* is not used in result clauses – a factor which helps to distinguish between purpose and result clauses, at least when they are negative.

ii) after **est/sunt** used in the sense of '**There is/are**':
multi sunt qui foedera rumpant.
'There are many people (of the type) who break agreements.'

iii) after **nemo**, **nullus**, **unus**, **solus**:
solus est qui hoc ius iurandum conservet.
'He is the only one (of the sort) who keeps this oath.'

iv) after **dignus/indignus**; translate 'worthy to...':
noster deus dignus est qui plurimos maximosque honores accipiat.
'Our god is worthy to receive many great tokens of respect.'

The words enclosed in brackets in the above translations reveal the slight difference between ordinary, purely adjectival relative clauses (normally containing indicative verbs) and these generic result clauses (containing subjunctive verbs). It is not always absolutely necessary to add these words to your translation [consider ii) above, for example, where even without these extra words it is reasonably clear that the antecedent describes a type of person]. In other contexts [consider i) above], the addition of these words offers a more faithful translation of the original Latin. Context, therefore, should dictate whether to express precisely the fact that the antecedent is viewed as a type or to leave this implicit. [Students working at **Level Two** or above may also find it useful to refer to **Chapter 10**.]

Exercises for Level One

Exercise 1A

The purpose and result clauses in these sentences appear in the same order as the descriptions above, with repetitions.

a) aliqui togam longissimam induunt ut divitias ostentent.
b) mater cultrum infanti abstulit ne sibi ipsi noceret.
c) Hannibal elephantos attulit qui se suosque suaque omnia trans Alpes transportarent.
d) imperatores Phidippiden Athenis misere qui Lacedaemoniorum auxilium in proelio Marathonio peteret.
e) Demosthenes os lapillis implebat quo clarius pronuntiare disceret.
f) Britanni se vitro inficiunt quo horridiores in pugna videantur.
g) Orpheus tanta dulcedine canebat ut omnia animalia moverentur.
h) Verres se tali furore gerebat ut omnes eum timerent.
i) rem agebat ea temeritate quae detrimentum inferre soleret.
j) multi sunt qui nimis temporis in convivio terant.

Exercise 1B[V]

a) sunt liberi qui numquam parentibus pareant.
b) illi libri digni sunt qui legantur.
c) Ulixes tam callidus erat ut Ilium dolis eius periret.
d) tanto dolore vidua commota est ut se in rogum iaceret.
e) aegrotus duo menses in cubili iacebat ut corpus ex morbo gravi reficeret.
f) Pelias Aesoniden per multa freta misit qui auream pellem reportaret.
g) Iasonne artibus magicis virginis fretus erat ut terrigenas pelleret?

h) aliqui philosophi artus exercent quo saniores mentis fiant.
i) nemo est qui numquam moriatur.
j) imperator insidias comparat quo melius impetum hostium moretur.

Exercise 1C(i)

Women are often dominant personalities.

['Why are you surprised, if a woman controls my life?...']

Colchis[5] flagrantes adamantina sub iuga tauros
egit et armigera proelia sevit humo,
custodisque feros clausit serpentis hiatus,
iret ut Aesonias aurea lana domos.
ausa ferox ab equo quondam oppugnare sagittis
Maeotis Danaum Penthesilea rates,
aurea cui postquam nudavit cassida frontem,
vicit victorem candida forma virum.
Omphale in **tantum** formae processit honorem,
Lydia Gygaeo tincta puella lacu,
ut, **qui**[6] pacato **statuisset** in orbe columnas,
tam dura **traheret** mollia pensa manu.

Propertius, *Elegies*

---

[5] *Colchis*: 'the Colchian maiden', i.e. 'Medea'.

[6] *qui*: using the number and gender of the pronoun as a guide, supply as the antecedent *is*, 'he, who…'; i.e. Hercules.

Exercise 1C(ii)

Tibullus bewails his servitude to a woman.

sic mihi seruitium uideo dominamque paratam:
    iam mihi, libertas illa paterna, uale.
seruitium sed triste datur, teneorque catenis,
    et numquam misero uincla remittit Amor,
et seu quid merui seu nil peccauimus, urit.
    uror: io, remoue, saeua puella, faces.

o ego **ne possim** tales sentire dolores,
    quam mallem[7] in gelidis montibus esse lapis!
stare uel insanis cautes obnoxia uentis,
    naufraga **quam** uasti **tunderet** unda maris!
nunc et amara dies et noctis amarior umbra est;
    omnia nunc tristi tempora felle madent.
nec prosunt elegi nec carminis auctor Apollo:
    illa caua pretium flagitat usque manu.

Tibullus, *Elegies*

---

[7] *quam mallem*: 'how I would prefer'.

Exercises for Level Two

Exercise 2A

a) nil erit ulterius quod nostris moribus addat
posteritas: eadem facient cupientque minores. (Juvenal)

b) duae sunt artes, quae possint locare homines in amplissimo gradu dignitatis, una imperatoris, altera oratoris boni. (Cicero)

c) quis est autem quem non moveat clarissimis monumentis testata consignataque antiquitas? (Cicero)

d) rure levis verno flores apis ingerit alveo,
compleat ut dulci sedula melle favos. (Tibullus)

e) M. Metilius tribunus plebis [dicit]...dictatorem...sedulo tempus terere quo diutius in magistratu sit solusque et Romae et in exercitu imperium habeat. (Livy)

f) mors misera non est commori cum quo velis. (Seneca)

g) veniet Phrygia iam pastor ab Ida,
qui gemitus irasque pares et mutua Grais
dona ferat. (Valerius Flaccus)

h) eo enim iam dementiae venimus ut qui parce adulatur pro maligno sit. (Seneca)

i) nulla fere causa est in qua non femina litem
moverit. (Juvenal)

j) quotus enim quisque tam patiens, ut velit discere, quod in usu non sit habiturus? (Pliny)

Exercise 2B(i)

The Assyrians first established divination as a science.

gentem quidem nullam video neque tam humanam atque doctam neque tam immanem atque barbaram, **quae** non significari futura et a quibusdam intellegi praedicique posse **censeat**. principio Assyrii, **ut** ab ultimis auctoritatem **repetam**, propter planitiem magnitudinemque regionum, quas incolebant, cum[8] caelum ex omni parte patens atque apertum intuerentur, traiectiones motusque stellarum observitaverunt, quibus notatis, quid[9] cuique significaretur memoriae prodiderunt. qua in natione Chaldaei...diuturna observatione siderum scientiam putantur effecisse, **ut** praedici **posset** quid[10] cuique eventurum et quo quisque fato natus esset. Cicero, *De Divinatione*

Exercise 2B(ii)

In Rome the practice of divination takes many forms.

nec unum genus est divinationis publice privatimque celebratum. nam, **ut omittam** ceteros populos, noster quam[11] multa genera complexus est! principio huius urbis parens Romulus non solum auspicato urbem condidisse, sed ipse etiam optimus augur fuisse traditur. deinde auguribus et reliqui reges usi, et exactis regibus, nihil publice sine auspiciis nec domi nec militiae gerebatur. cumque[12] magna vis videretur esse et impetriendis[13] consulendisque rebus et monstris interpretandis ac procurandis in haruspicum disciplina, omnem hanc ex Etruria scientiam adhibebant, **ne** genus **esset** ullum divinationis, **quod** neglectum ab eis **videretur**. Cicero, *De Divinatione*

---

[8] *cum...intuerentur*: see **4. Temporal Conjunctions E** vi).

[9] *quid...significaretur*: see **2. Indirect Speech Part 6**.

[10] *quid...eventurum (esset) et quo...fato...natus esset*: see **2. Indirect Speech Part 6**.

[11] *quam multa...*: 'how many...'.

[12] *cum...videretur*: see **4. Temporal Conjunctions E** vi).

[13] *impetriendis consulendisque...procurandis*: see **5. Gerunds and Gerundives D** d).

Exercise 2C

Catullus longs to be with Licinius Calvus again.

hesterno, Licini, die otiosi
multum lusimus in meis tabellis,
ut conuenerat esse delicatos:
scribens uersiculos uterque nostrum
ludebat numero modo hoc modo illoc,
reddens mutua per iocum atque uinum.
atque illinc abii tuo lepore
incensus, Licini, facetiisque,
ut nec me miserum cibus **iuuaret**
nec somnus **tegeret** quiete ocellos,
sed toto indomitus furore lecto
uersarer, cupiens uidere lucem,
ut tecum **loquerer** simulque **ut essem**.
at defessa labore membra postquam
semimortua lectulo iacebant,
hoc, iucunde, tibi poema feci,
ex **quo perspiceres** meum dolorem.
nunc audax caue[14] sis, precesque nostras,
oramus, caue despuas, ocelle,
ne poenas Nemesis **reposcat** a te.
est uemens dea: laedere hanc caueto.

Catullus

[14] *caue sis...caue despuas*: 'beware lest you are...beware lest you despise...'.

Exercises for Level Three

Exercise 3A

Overcome by grief Catullus cannot help Manius.

quod mihi fortuna casuque oppressus acerbo
conscriptum hoc lacrimis mittis epistolium,
naufragum **ut** eiectum spumantibus aequoris undis
subleuem et a mortis limine **restituam**,
quem neque sancta Venus molli requiescere somno
desertum in lecto caelibe perpetitur,
nec ueterum dulci scriptorum carmine Musae
oblectant, cum mens anxia peruigilat:
id gratum est mihi, me quoniam tibi dicis amicum,
muneraque et Musarum hinc petis et Veneris.
sed tibi **ne** mea **sint** ignota incommoda, Mani,
neu me odisse **putes** hospitis officium,
accipe, quis merser fortunae fluctibus ipse,
ne amplius a misero dona beata **petas**.
tempore quo primum uestis mihi tradita pura est,
iucundum cum aetas florida uer ageret,
multa satis lusi: non est dea nescia nostri,
quae dulcem curis miscet amaritiem.
sed totum hoc studium luctu fraterna mihi mors
abstulit. o misero frater adempte mihi,
tu mea tu moriens fregisti commoda, frater,
tecum una tota est nostra sepulta domus,
omnia tecum una perierunt gaudia nostra,
quae tuus in uita dulcis alebat amor.

Catullus

Exercise 3B

Pliny approves of Colonus' sincere grief.

C. PLINIUS COLONO SUO S.

unice probo quod Pompei Quintiani morte **tam** dolenter adficeris, **ut** amissi caritatem desiderio **extendas**, non ut plerique qui tantum viventes amant seu potius amare se simulant, ac ne simulant quidem nisi quos florentes vident; nam miserorum non secus ac defunctorum obliviscuntur. sed tibi perennis fides **tanta**que in amore constantia, **ut** finiri nisi tua morte non **possit**. et hercule is fuit Quintianus, **quem** diligi **deceat** ipsius exemplo. felices amabat, miseros tuebatur, desiderabat amissos. iam illa quanta probitas in ore, quanta in sermone cunctatio, quam pari libra gravitas comitasque! quod studium litterarum, quod iudicium! qua pietate cum dissimillimo patre vivebat! quam non obstabat illi, quo minus[15] vir optimus videretur, quod erat optimus filius! sed quid dolorem tuum exulcero? quamquam **sic** amasti iuvenem **ut** hoc potius quam de illo sileri **velis**, a me praesertim, cuius praedicatione putas vitam eius ornari, memoriam prorogari, ipsamque illam qua est raptus aetatem posse restitui. vale.

Pliny, *Letters*

---

[15] *quo minus*: see **7. Verbs of Fearing/quominus & quin Part 2 A** i).

Exercises for Level Four

Exercise 4A

Advice on how to pray wisely.

nil ergo optabunt homines? si consilium vis,
permittes ipsis expendere numinibus quid
conveniat nobis rebusque sit utile nostris.
nam pro iucundis aptissima quaeque dabunt di:
carior est illis homo quam sibi. nos animorum
inpulsu et caeca magnaque cupidine ducti
coniugium petimus partumque uxoris; at illis
notum qui pueri qualisque futura sit uxor.
ut tamen et **poscas** aliquid **voveas**que sacellis
exta et candiduli divina tomacula porci,
orandum est ut sit mens sana in corpore sano;
fortem posce animum mortis terrore carentem,
qui spatium vitae extremum inter munera **ponat**
naturae, **qui** ferre **queat** quoscumque labores,
nesciat irasci, **cupiat** nihil et potiores
Herculis aerumnas **credat** saevosque labores
et venere et cenis et pluma Sardanapalli.
monstro quod ipse tibi possis dare; semita certe
tranquillae per virtutem patet unica vitae.
nullum numen habes, si sit prudentia: nos te,
nos facimus, Fortuna, deam caeloque locamus.

Juvenal, *Satires*

Exercise 4B

Hannibal's undying enmity towards the Romans.

hic autem uelut hereditate relictum odium paternum erga Romanos **sic** conseruauit, **ut** prius animam quam id **deposuerit**, qui quidem, cum patria pulsus esset et alienarum opum indigeret, numquam destiterit animo bellare cum Romanis. nam **ut omittam** Philippum, quem absens hostem reddidit Romanis, omnium iis temporibus potentissimus rex Antiochus fuit. hunc **tanta** cupiditate incendit bellandi, **ut** usque a rubro mari arma **conatus sit** inferre Italiae. ad quem cum legati uenissent Romani, **qui** de eius uoluntate **explorarent darentque** operam consiliis clandestinis **ut** Hannibalem in suspicionem regi **adducerent**, tamquam ab ipsis corruptum alia atque antea sentire, neque id frustra fecissent idque Hannibal comperisset seque ab interioribus consiliis segregari uidisset, tempore dato adiit ad regem, eique cum multa de fide sua et odio in Romanos commemorasset, hoc adiunxit: 'pater meus' inquit 'Hamilcar puerulo me, utpote non amplius nouem annos nato, in Hispaniam imperator proficiscens Karthagine Ioui optimo maximo hostias immolauit. quae diuina res dum conficiebatur, quaesiuit a me uellemne secum in castra proficisci. id cum libenter accepissem atque ab eo petere coepissem ne dubitaret ducere, tum ille "faciam" inquit, "si mihi fidem quam postulo dederis." simul me ad aram adduxit, apud quam sacrificare instituerat, eamque ceteris remotis tenentem iurare iussit numquam me in amicitia cum Romanis fore. id ego iusiurandum patri datum usque ad hanc aetatem **ita** conseruaui, **ut** nemini dubium esse **debeat**, quin reliquo tempore eadem mente sim futurus. quare si quid amice de Romanis cogitabis, non imprudenter feceris, si me celaris; cum quidem bellum parabis, te ipsum frustraberis, si non me in eo principem posueris.'

Cornelius Nepos

Exercises for Level Five

Exercise 5A

Memorization of words is a useful, transferable skill.

nunc, ne forte verborum memoriam aut nimis difficilem aut parum utilem arbitrere, rerum ipsarum memoria contentus sis, quod et utilior sit et plus habeat facultatis, admonendus es quare verborum memoriam non inprobemus. nam putamus oportere eos, qui velint res faciliores sine labore et molestia facere, in rebus difficilioribus esse ante exercitatos. nec nos hanc verborum memoriam inducimus ut versus meminisse possimus, sed ut hac exercitatione illa rerum memoria, quae pertinet ad utilitatem, confirmetur, ut ab hac difficili consuetudine sine labore ad illam facultatem transire possimus. sed cum in omni disciplina infirma est artis praeceptio sine summa adsiduitate exercitationis, tum vero in mnemonicis minimum valet doctrina, nisi industria, studio, labore, diligentia conprobatur. quam plurimos locos ut habeas et quam maxime ad praecepta adcommodatos curare poteris; in imaginibus conlocandis exerceri cotidie convenit. non enim, sicut a ceteris studiis abducimur nonnumquam occupatione, item ab hac re nos potest causa deducere aliqua. numquam est enim quin aliquid memoriae tradere velimus, et tum maxime cum aliquo maiore negotio detinemur. quare, cum sit utile facile meminisse, non te fallit quod tantopere utile sit quanto labore sit appetendum; quod poteris existimare utilitate cognita. pluribus verbis ad eam te hortari non est sententia, ne aut tuo studio diffisi aut minus quam res postulat dixisse videamur.

Ad Herennium

Exercise 5B

The Rise and 'Fall' of Eloquence.

age uero, urbibus constitutis, ut fidem colere et iustitiam retinere discerent et aliis parere sua uoluntate consuescerent ac non modo labores excipiendos communis commodi causa, sed etiam uitam amittendam existimarent, qui tandem fieri potuit, nisi homines ea quae ratione inuenissent eloquentia persuadere potuissent? profecto nemo nisi graui ac suaui commotus oratione, cum uiribus plurimum posset, ad ius uoluisset sine ui descendere, ut inter quos posset excellere, cum iis se pateretur aequari et sua uoluntate a iucundissima consuetudine recederet, quae praesertim iam naturae uim optineret propter uetustatem. ac primo quidem sic et nata et progressa longius eloquentia uidetur et item postea maximis in rebus pacis et belli cum summis hominum utilitatibus esse uersata; postquam uero commoditas quaedam, praua uirtutis imitatrix, sine ratione officii dicendi copiam consecuta est, tum ingenio freta malitia peruertere urbes et uitas hominum labefactare assueuit. atque huius quoque exordium mali, quoniam principium boni diximus, explicemus. ueri simillimum mihi uidetur quodam tempore neque in publicis rebus infantes et insipientes homines solitos esse uersari nec uero ad priuatas causas magnos ac dissertos homines accedere, sed cum a summis uiris maximae res administrarentur, arbitror alios fuisse non incallidos homines qui ad paruas controuersias priuatorum accederent. quibus in controuersiis cum saepe a mendacio contra uerum stare homines consuescerent, dicendi assiduitas induit audaciam, ut necessario superiores illi propter iniurias ciuium resistere audacibus et opitulari suis quisque necessariis cogeretur. itaque cum in dicendo saepe par, nonnumquam etiam superior uisus esset is qui, omisso studio sapientiae, nihil sibi praeter eloquentiam comparasset, fiebat ut et multitudinis et suo iudicio dignus qui rem publicam gereret uideretur. hinc nimirum non iniuria, cum ad gubernacula rei publicae temerarii atque audaces homines accesserant, maxima ac miserrima naufragia fiebant. quibus rebus tantum odii atque inuidiae suscepit eloquentia ut homines ingeniosissimi, quasi ex aliqua turbida tempestate in portum, sic ex seditiosa ac tumultuosa uita se in studium aliquod traderent quietum.

Cicero, *De Inventione*

Chapter 7

VERBS OF FEARING/QUOMINUS AND QUIN

Parallel Revision: Present Subjunctives, Kennedy 115-25, 133-41, *CLG* 7d-e, 8b, 9.2, *OLG* pp. 37-60.

Part 1. Verbs of Fearing

There are **three** constructions used with verbs of fearing (the most common of which are *timeo*, *metuo* and *vereor*):

i) a direct object in the **accusative**, 'I am afraid **of** something':

mortem timeo.
'I am afraid of death.'

ii) the **infinitive**, 'I am afraid **to do** something':

in proelium inire metuo.
'I am afraid to enter battle.'

iii) ***ne*** followed by a **subjunctive**, to indicate a **positive** fear: 'that (lest) something **might** happen';

or ***ut***, occasionally (***ne...non***), with a subjunctive, to indicate a **negative** fear: 'that (lest) something **might not** happen':[1]

*metuo **ne** hostes nos adgrediantur.*
'I am afraid that the enemy **might** attack us.'
*vereor **ut** Iuppiter nobis adsit.*
'I am afraid that Jupiter **might not** help us.'
*timeo **ne** nostri milites hostes **non** superent.*
'I am afraid that our soldiers **might not** overcome the enemy.'

---

[1] Some nouns expressing anxiety or fear (e.g., *timor, pavor* etc.) may also take this construction.

Students working at Level One should now attempt Exercise 1A^V on p. 114.

Part 2: *quominus* & *quin*

A. *quominus* takes a **subjunctive** verb. It occurs most commonly after verbs (and occasionally nouns[2]) of **hindering**, **preventing** etc. In this context, *quominus* is usually best translated as '**from doing**':

non ea res me deterruit, quominus litteras ad te mitterem. (Cicero)
'This matter did not deter me *from sending* a letter to you.'
quae (formido) tales viros impediat, quominus causam velint dicere. (Cicero)
'...which (fear) hinders such men *from wanting* to plead their case.'

Very occasionally, *quominus* occurs in two further contexts:
i) in the context of **delaying**, **hesitating**, etc., in which it can be translated 'preventing x from *do*ing' or simply '**before doing**', '**before x happens/happened**' etc.:

Caesar nihil in mora habuit, quominus perveniret... (Velleius)
'Caesar experienced no delay *before arriving.../preventing him from arriving...*'

ii) in the phrase **per aliquem stat quominus...**, meaning 'it is x's responsibility/fault that y is NOT happening':

Caesar...cognovit per Afranium stare, quominus proelio dimicaretur. (Caesar)
'Caesar...realised that it was Afranius' fault that a battle was not taking place.'

---

[2] Typical nouns taking this construction include both *mora* 'delay' and *impedimentum* 'hindrance', both of which occur in predicative dative expressions. See **3. Predicative Datives**.

B. Coping with *quin*: the first step

quin is found with both indicative and subjunctive verbs. Since the meaning of *quin* is dependent on the mood which follows it, it is essential to identify this mood before attempting to translate.

C. *quin* + indicative

quin occurs with the indicative in three main uses:

i) introducing direct questions in the sense of '**Why... not...?**' or '**How...not...?**'
quin potius pacem aeternam pactosque hymenaeos exercemus? (Virgil)
'Why do we not rather busy ourselves with eternal peace and the pledged marriage?'

ii) in the corrective sense of '**no, rather**'; in this sense *quin* is often found in conjunction with *potius* or *contra*:
Phidias statuas pulchras summa arte fecit; quin potius multo pulcherrimas omnium finxit.
'Phidias made beautiful statues with supreme skill; no, rather, he made by far the most beautiful of all.'

iii) as a (polite) expletive (i.e. a word which has no real meaning of its own, but which adds emphasis or colour); in this sense *quin* is either found on its own or with *et* (in the sense of 'also'), *etiam*, *igitur*, an imperative or jussive subjunctive:[3]
quin sic attendite, iudices. (Cicero)
'So, pay attention thus, judges.'

---

[3] For jussive subjunctives, see **8. Independent Subjunctives B** i).

D. *quin* + subjunctive[4]

quin also introduces four common types of clause using a subjunctive verb. Three of these occur in very specific contexts. The key to coping with *quin* + subjunctive is in fact to identify the context in which it exists: if it is that specified below in i) or ii) or iii), follow the guidelines given for the translation of each; if the context conforms to none of these, translate according to the advice given in iv).

i) like *quominus, quin* is used after verbs (or occasionally nouns) of **hindering/preventing** etc. or, occasionally, after verbs of **delaying** etc. As with *quominus*, after verbs of hindering or preventing etc., *quin* is best translated '**from doing**' and, after verbs of delaying, '**before doing**'/ '**before x happens**' etc..

> *ego vix teneor, quin accurram.* (Cicero)
> 'I am scarcely restrained from coming quickly.'
> *nulla mora facta, quin Poenus educeret in aciem copiamque pugnandi faceret.* (Livy)
> 'Nor was there any delay before the Carthaginian led them out into the battle line and gave an opportunity for fighting'.

ii) *quin* is frequently used in the context of **doubting**, in which case the translation 'but that' or (less stilted) '**that**' is usually appropriate:

> *haud dubito quin mentiaris.*
> 'I do not doubt (but) that you are lying.'

---

[4] *quin* + subjunctive differs in usage from *quominus* in that the clause by which it is governed must contain some form of negative (e.g. *non, nihil, nemo* etc.) or virtual negative (e.g. *vix* 'scarcely', *aegre* 'scarcely', *haud multum* 'not much').

iii) *quin* + subjunctive also occurs commonly as part of three phrases:

- ***haud multum abest*[5] *quin*** (with its many variations, e.g. *non procul abest quin, paulum abest quin*): literally 'it is not far from x *do*ing', which may be rendered more fluently '**x very nearly (happens)**'; use the literal translation to establish the correct sense and then re-adjust your translation:
  onere equi super eum ruentis haud multum afuit quin exanimaretur. (Livy)
  'with the weight of the horse falling on him it was not far from him being deprived of breath', i.e. 'with the weight of the horse falling on him he was very nearly suffocated.'
- ***non possum quin***: '**I cannot but**'.
- ***nulla causa est quin***: '**There is no reason why...not...**'.

iv) if *quin* occurs in a context different from those defined above, translate either '**without doing**' or '**but that...**' or '**that...not**' or '**who/which...not**', as appropriate to the context; if the use of these phrases results in a stilted translation, having established the correct sense, adjust your translation to create fluent English:

...neque vero quisquam potest hostis advolare terra, quin eum... adesse...scire possimus. (Cicero)
'...nor indeed can any enemy arrive by land, without our being able to realise that he is there.'
ecquis fuit, quin lacrimaret, quin putaret...? (Cicero)
'Was there anyone, who did not cry, who did not think...?'

---

5 *abest* in this context is always impersonal, i.e. 'it is (far) from...'

Exercises for Level One

Exercise 1A^{V}: Verbs of Fearing

a) timeo ne hostes nos fugent.
b) veriti in aperto fugere, multi se in tenebris celabant.
c) uxor timet ne vir vixerit.
d) Hecuba metuebat ne capta vinciretur inque servitutem abduceretur.
e) imperator verebatur ne seditionem non vinceret.
f) virgines inire in lucum metuebant.
g) timeo ne mox lucem amittam.
h) Antigone timebat ne fratris corpus ferae distraherent.
i) paterfamilias metuit ne ignavia filii familiae dedecus ferat.
j) Turnus timet ne Aeneas extremum ictum feriat.

Exercise 1B: *quominus & quin*

a) nihil nos impediet quin Romam regrediamur.
b) haud dubium est quin reus nocens sit.
c) hiems gravis nautas prohibuit quominus se a naufragio servarent.
d) nemo hodie dubitat quin terra rotunda sit.
e) nulla mora erat quin proelio decertaretur.
f) nemo erat quin statuam verisimillimam miraretur.
g) haud multum afuit quin hostes omnis aras sanctissimas violarent.
h) fata obstant quominus Aeneas Carthagini maneat.
i) non potes quin verum confitearis.
j) nulli fures ingredi poterunt quin cardine crepitante audiantur.

Exercise 1C

Has the astrologer's prediction concerning Munna come true?

dixerat astrologus periturum[6] te cito, Munna,
nec, puto, mentitus dixerat ille tibi.
nam tu dum[7] **metuis ne** quid post fata **relinquas**,
hausisti patrias luxuriosus opes,
bisque tuum deciens non toto tabuit anno.
dic mihi, non hoc est, Munna, perire cito?

Martial

Exercise 1D

Body, mind and soul are inextricably linked.

haec igitur natura[8] tenetur corpore ab omni
ipsaque corporis est custos et causa salutis;
nam communibus inter se radicibus haerent
nec sine pernicie divelli posse videntur.
quod genus[9] e thuris glaebis evellere odorem
haud facile est **quin intereat** natura quoque eius,
sic animi atque animae naturam corpore toto
extrahere haud facile est **quin** omnia **dissolvantur**.

Lucretius, *De Rerum Natura*

---

[6] *periturum te*: see **2. Indirect Speech Part 2**.
[7] *dum metuis*: see **4. Temporal Conjunctions F** i).
[8] *haec...natura*: 'This nature', i.e. body, mind and soul.
[9] *quod genus*: 'just as...'.

Exercises for Level Two

Exercise 2A

a) numquam est enim quin aliquid memoriae tradere velimus. (*Ad Herennium*)

b) quoniam haec est vita... quid moror in terris? quin huc ad vos venire propero? (Cicero)

c) certa quidem finis vitae mortalibus adstat,
nec devitari letum pote quin obeamus. (Lucretius)

d) non causam dico quin quod meritus sit ferat. (Terence)

e) nemo est tam fortis quin rei novitate perturbetur. (Caesar)

f) quis dubitare, mi Lucili, potest quin deorum immortalium munus sit quod vivimus, philosophiae quod bene vivimus? (Seneca)

g) [Io] metuitque loqui, ne more iuvencae
mugiat... (Ovid)

h) nec morati sunt quin decurrerent, sicut imperatum erat, ad castra. (Livy)

i) quis dubitat quin in aeternum urbe condita, in immensum crescente nova imperia, sacerdotia, iura gentium hominumque instituantur? (Livy)

j) vereor ut satis diligenter actum in senatu sit de litteris meis. (Cicero)

Exercise 2B

Our ancestors surpassed us in virtue and wisdom.

maiores nostri, patres conscripti, neque consili neque audaciae umquam eguere; neque illis superbia obstabat, **quo minus** aliena instituta, si modo proba erant, **imitarentur**. arma atque tela militaria ab Samnitibus, insignia magistratuum ab Tuscis pleraque sumpserunt. postremo, quod ubique apud socios aut hostis idoneum videbatur, cum summo studio domi exequebantur: imitari quam invidere bonis malebant. sed eodem illo tempore Graeciae morem imitati verberibus animadvortebant in civis, de condemnatis summum supplicium sumebant. postquam respublica adolevit et multitudine civium factiones valuere, circumveniri innocentes, alia huiuscemodi fieri coepere, tum lex Porcia aliaeque leges paratae sunt, quibus legibus exilium damnatis permissum est. hanc ego causam,[10] patres conscripti, **quo minus** novom consilium **capiamus**, in primis magnam puto. profecto virtus atque sapientia maior illis fuit, qui ex parvis opibus tantum imperium fecere, quam in nobis, qui ea bene parta vix retinemus.

Sallust, *Catilinae Coniuratio*

Exercise 2C

The Carthaginians suffer heavy losses near Munda.

ad Mundam exinde castra Punica mota et Romani eo confestim secuti sunt. ibi signis conlatis pugnatum per quattuor ferme horas egregieque uincentibus Romanis signum receptui est datum, quod Cn. Scipionis femur tragula confixum erat **pauor**que circa eum ceperat milites **ne** mortiferum **esset** uolnus. ceterum **haud dubium fuit quin**, nisi ea mora interuenisset,[11] castra eo die Punica capi **potuerint**; nam non milites solum sed elephanti etiam usque ad uallum acti erant, superque ipsas fossas nouem et triginta elephanti pilis confixi. hoc quoque proelio ad duodecim milia hominum dicuntur caesa, prope tria capta cum signis militaribus septem et quinquaginta.

Livy

---

[10] *causam*: 'a reason (preventing us...)'.

[11] *nisi...interuenisset*: see **9. Conditional Sentences C** iii).

Exercises for Level Three

Exercise 3A

Cicero sends Curio belated congratulations and advice to trust his own counsel.

sera gratulatio reprehendi non solet, praesertim si nulla neglegentia praetermissa est; longe enim absum, audio sero; sed tibi et gratulor et, ut sempiternae laudi tibi sit iste tribunatus, exopto teque hortor, ut omnia gubernes et moderere prudentia tua, ne te auferant aliorum consilia. nemo est qui tibi sapientius suadere possit te ipso; numquam labere, si te audies. non scribo hoc temere; cui scribam, video; novi animum, novi consilium tuum; non **vereor ne** quid timide, ne quid stulte facias, si ea defendes, quae ipse recta esse senties. quod[12] in rei publicae tempus non incideris, sed veneris (iudicio enim tuo, non casu in ipsum discrimen rerum contulisti tribunatum tuum), profecto vides; quanta vis in re publica temporum sit, quanta varietas rerum, quam incerti exitus, quam flexibiles hominum voluntates, quid insidiarum, quid vanitatis in vita, **non dubito quin** cogites. sed, amabo te, cura et cogita, Curio,-nihil novi, sed illud idem, quod initio scripsi: tecum loquere, te adhibe in consilium, te audi, tibi obtempera.

Cicero, *Letters*

Exercise 3B

A narrow escape from death.

nec aliud Radamisto subsidium fuit quam pernicitas equorum, quis seque et coniugem abstulit. sed coniunx gravida primam utcumque fugam ob metum hostilem et mariti caritatem toleravit; post festinatione continua, ubi quatitur uterus et viscera vibrantur, orare ut morte honesta

[12] *quod*: '(the fact) that'.

contumeliis captivitatis eximeretur. ille primo amplecti adlevare adhortari, modo virtutem admirans, modo **timore** aeger, **ne** quis relicta **poteretur**. postremo violentia amoris et facinorum non rudis destringit acinacen vulneratamque ripam ad Araxis trahit, flumini tradit, ut corpus etiam auferretur: ipse praeceps Hiberos ad patrium regnum pervadit. interim Zenobiam (id mulieri nomen) placida in eluvie spirantem ac vitae manifestam advertere pastores, et dignitate formae haud degenerem reputantes obligant vulnus, agrestia medicamina adhibent cognitoque nomine et casu in urbem Artaxata ferunt; unde publica cura deducta ad Tiridaten comiterque excepta culta regio habita est.

Tacitus, *Annals*

Exercise 3C

Fabius meets his death at the hands of Attius Varus' men.

sed praeoccupatus animus Attianorum militum timore et fuga et caede suorum nihil de resistendo cogitabat, omnesque iam se ab equitatu circumveniri arbitrabantur. itaque priusquam telum adigi posset aut nostri propius accederent, omnis Vari acies terga vertit seque in castra recepit. qua in fuga Fabius Paelignus quidam ex infimis ordinibus de exercitu Curionis primum agmen fugientium consecutus magna voce Varum nomine appellans requirebat, uti unus esse ex eius militibus et monere aliquid velle ac dicere videretur. ubi ille saepius appellatus aspexit ac restitit et quis esset aut quid vellet quaesivit, umerum apertum gladio appetit **paulumque afuit quin** Varum **interficeret**; quod ille periculum sublato ad eius conatum scuto vitavit. Fabius a proximis militibus circumventus interficitur.

Caesar, *Bellum Civile*

Exercises for Level Four

Exercise 4A

Cato uses Nestor as an example of the value of an old man.

videtisne ut apud Homerum saepissime Nestor de virtutibus suis praedicet? tertiam enim iam aetatem hominum vivebat, nec erat ei **verendum ne** vera praedicans de se nimis videretur aut insolens aut loquax. etenim, ut ait Homerus, 'ex eius lingua melle dulcior fluebat oratio'; quam ad suavitatem nullis egebat corporis viribus: et tamen dux ille Graeciae nusquam optat ut Aiacis similes habeat decem, at ut Nestoris, quod si acciderit, non **dubitat quin** brevi sit Troia peritura. sed redeo ad me. quartum annum ago et octogesimum: vellem equidem idem posse gloriari quod Cyrus; sed tamen hoc queo dicere, non me quidem eis esse viribus quibus aut miles bello Punico aut quaestor eodem bello aut consul in Hispania fuerim, aut quadriennio post cum tribunus militaris depugnavi apud Thermopylas M'. Acilio Glabrione consule; sed tamen, ut vos videtis, non plane me enervavit, non adflixit senectus: non curia vires meas desiderat, non rostra, non amici, non clientes, non hospites. nec enim unquam sum assensus veteri illi laudatoque proverbio quod monet mature fieri senem, si diu velis esse senex. ego vero me minus diu senem esse mallem quam esse senem ante quam essem.

Cicero, *De Senectute*

Exercise 4B

Death will have no sting, if Cynthia remains true to her love.

non ego nunc tristes **vereor**, mea Cynthia, **Manes**,
nec moror extremo debita fata rogo,
sed **ne** forte tuo **careat** mihi funus amore,
hic **timor** est ipsis durior exsequiis.
non adeo leviter noster puer haesit ocellis,
ut meus oblito pulvis amore vacet.
illic Phylacides iucundae coniugis heros
non potuit caecis immemor esse locis,
sed cupidus falsis attingere gaudia palmis
Thessalus antiquam venerat umbra domum.
illic, quidquid ero, semper tua dicar imago:
traicit et fati litora magnus amor.
illic formosae veniant chorus heroinae,
quas dedit Argivis Dardana praeda viris,
quarum nulla tua fuerit mihi, Cynthia, forma
gratior, et (Tellus hoc ita iusta sinat)
quamvis te longae remorentur fata senectae,
cara tamen lacrimis ossa futura meis.
quae tu viva mea possis sentire favilla
tum mihi non ullo mors sit amara loco.
quam **vereor ne** te contempto, Cynthia, busto
abstrahat a nostro pulvere iniquus Amor,
cogat et invitam lacrimas siccare cadentes!
flectitur assiduis certa puella minis.
quare, dum licet, inter nos laetemur amantes:
non satis est ullo tempore longus amor.

Propertius, *Elegies*

Exercise 4C

The besieged and the besiegers abandon active hostilities pending the arrival of Caesar.

ubi hostes ad legatos exercitumque pervenerunt, universi se ad pedes proiciunt; orant ut adventus Caesaris exspectetur: captam suam urbem videre, opera perfecta, turrim subrutam; itaque ab defensione desistere; nullam exoriri moram posse **quominus**, cum venisset, si imperata non facerent ad nutum, e vestigio **diriperentur**. docent, si omnino turris concidisset, non posse milites contineri **quin** spe praedae in urbem **irrumperent** urbemque **delerent**. haec atque eiusdem generis complura ut ab hominibus doctis magna cum misericordia fletuque pronuntiantur. quibus rebus commoti legati milites ex opere deducunt, oppugnatione desistunt; operibus custodias relinquunt. indutiarum quodam genere misericordia facto adventus Caesaris exspectatur. nullum ex muro, nullum a nostris mittitur telum; ut re confecta omnes curam et diligentiam remittunt. Caesar enim per litteras Trebonio magnopere mandaverat, ne per vim oppidum expugnari pateretur, ne gravius permoti milites et defectionis odio et contemptione sui et diutino labore omnis puberes interficerent; quod se facturos minabantur aegreque tunc sunt retenti **quin** oppidum **irrumperent**, graviterque eam rem tulerunt, quod stetisse per Trebonium **quominus** oppido **potirentur** videbatur.

Caesar, *Bellum Civile*

Exercises for Level Five

Exercise 5A

Nero and the great fire of Rome.

eo in tempore Nero Antii agens non ante in urbem regressus est quam domui eius, qua Palatium et Maecenatis hortos continuaverat, ignis propinquaret. neque tamen sisti potuit, quin et Palatium et domus et cuncta circum haurirentur. sed solacium populo exturbato ac profugo campum Martis ac monumenta Agrippae, hortos quin etiam suos patefecit et subitaria aedificia exstruxit, quae multitudinem inopem acciperent; subvectaque utensilia ab Ostia et propinquis municipiis, pretiumque frumenti minutum usque ad ternos nummos. quae quamquam popularia in inritum cadebant, quia pervaserat rumor ipso tempore flagrantis urbis inisse eum domesticam scaenam et cecinisse Troianum excidium, praesentia mala vetustis cladibus adsimulantem...

[Nero profits from the fire by the rebuilding of his own palace and special landscaping of his gardens. However, he foots the bill for the rebuilding of the rest of Rome and prescribes measures to avoid any future fires on a similar scale and to appease the gods.]

sed non ope humana, non largitionibus principis aut deum placamentis decedebat infamia, quin iussum incendium crederetur. ergo abolendo rumori Nero subdidit reos et quaesitissimis poenis adfecit, quos per flagitia invisos vulgus Christianos appellabat. auctor nominis eius Christus Tiberio imperitante per procuratorem Pontium Pilatum supplicio adfectus erat; repressaque in praesens exitiabilis superstitio rursum erumpebat, non modo per Iudaeam, originem eius mali, sed per urbem etiam, quo cuncta undique atrocia aut pudenda confluunt celebranturque. igitur primum correpti qui fatebantur, deinde indicio eorum multitudo ingens haud perinde in crimine incendii quam odio humani generis convicti sunt.

Tacitus, *Annals*

Exercise 5B

Marius was sensible not to attend the recent theatrical spectacles.

M. CICERO S. D. M. MARIO.

si te dolor aliqui corporis aut infirmitas valetudinis tuae tenuit quo minus ad ludos venires, fortunae magis tribuo quam sapientiae tuae; sin haec, quae ceteri mirantur, contemnenda duxisti et, cum per valetudinem posses, venire tamen noluisti, utrumque laetor, et sine dolore corporis te fuisse et animo valuisse, cum ea, quae sine causa mirantur alii, neglexeris, modo ut tibi constiterit fructus oti tui; quo quidem tibi perfrui mirifice licuit, cum esses in ista amoenitate paene solus relictus. neque tamen dubito quin tu in illo cubiculo tuo, ex quo tibi Stabianum perforasti et patefecisti sinum, per eos dies matutina tempora lectiunculis consumpseris, cum illi interea, qui te istic reliquerunt, spectarent communis mimos semisomni. reliquas vero partis diei tu consumebas iis delectationibus, quas tibi ipse ad arbitrium tuum compararas; nobis autem erant ea perpetienda, quae Sp. Maecius probavisset. omnino, si quaeris, ludi apparatissimi, sed non tui stomachi; coniecturam enim facio de meo. nam primum honoris causa in scaenam redierant ii, quos ego honoris causa de scaena decessisse arbitrabar. deliciae vero tuae, noster Aesopus, eius modi fuit ut ei desinere per omnis homines liceret. is iurare cum coepisset, vox eum defecit in illo loco: 'si sciens fallo.' quid tibi ego alia narrem? nosti enim reliquos ludos; qui ne id quidem leporis habuerunt, quod solent mediocres ludi. apparatus enim spectatio tollebat omnem hilaritatem, quo quidem apparatu non dubito quin animo aequissimo carueris. quid enim delectationis habent sescenti muli in 'Clytaemestra' aut in 'Equo Troiano' creterrarum tria milia aut armatura varia peditatus et equitatus in aliqua pugna? quae popularem admirationem habuerunt, delectationem tibi nullam attulissent.

Cicero, *Letters*

Chapter 8

INDEPENDENT SUBJUNCTIVES

Parallel Revision: Perfect Subjunctives, Kennedy 115-25, *CLG* 7d-e, 8b, 9.2, *OLG* pp. 37-60.

A. What are Independent Subjunctives?

All the subjunctives that we have considered so far have occurred in the context of subordinate clauses, e.g. in purpose and result clauses, certain temporal clauses, etc. In the context of these subordinate clauses, the origin of the term 'subjunctive' is readily apparent, i.e. a verb used (most often) in clauses 'joined to' a main clause, from the Latin *subiungo* 'to join to' or 'to add to'.

Sometimes, however, **subjunctives occur as the main verb of a sentence**. Subjunctives of this nature are called 'independent subjunctives'. Subjunctives are in fact just one of the three general sub-divisions of verbs called 'moods', the other two moods being the indicative and the imperative. Each of these three moods can be used as the main verb of a sentence, with each having its own specific function:

i) an **indicative** verb is used where the speaker wishes **to represent a statement or question as fact** (the statement need not in reality be factual, but the speaker nevertheless wishes to portray it as such): so, the statement 'Latin is a living language' would be constructed using the indicative *est*.

ii) an **imperative** is used **to issue a positive command** (usually to a second person or persons, 'you'[1]); so, 'Speak!' would be translated *dic!* or *dicite!*.

---

[1] Imperatives in the third person also exist (see Kennedy 115-24), but occur extremely rarely in extant Latin literature.

iii) broadly speaking, a **subjunctive** is used in a main clause where the speaker wishes to portray **a statement or question as conditional/ hypothetical, willed or desired**.

The rest of this chapter will consider those independent subjunctives whose function is to portray a statement or question as willed or desired. For those independent subjunctives presenting a statement or question as conditional/hypothethical, see the following chapter on **Conditional Sentences**.

B. Jussive Subjunctives

i) Latin does not have imperative forms for first person subjects (i.e. 'I', 'we') and those for third person subjects (i.e. 'he/she/it' and 'they') are extremely rare. So, Latin uses a **present subjunctive**, a so-called 'jussive subjunctive',[2] to issue orders, commands or exhortations to these subjects,[3] with *ne* added where a negative is required. Translate a first person jussive subjunctive '**let me...**' or '**let us...**', as appropriate, and a third person jussive subjunctive '**let him/her/it...**' or '**let them...**':

superstitiones exitialis aboleamus!
'Let us abolish destructive superstitions!'
me timeant!
'Let them fear me!'
ne domum regrediantur!
'Don't let them return home!'

---

[2] The term 'jussive' is derived from the Latin *iubeo* (cf. the perfect participle *iussus*), meaning 'I order'.

[3] Very occasionally, present subjunctives are also used in the second person (i.e. 'you' forms) to issue such a command/exhortation.

ii) Latin does not normally use imperative forms where a command is negative, i.e. 'Don't…!'.[4] Instead, Latin uses either *noli/nolite* + infinitive or a second type of jussive subjunctive, i.e. **ne with a perfect subjunctive**:

ne dolueritis!
'Don't be upset!'
ne oblitus sis!
'Don't forget!'.

C. Deliberative Subjunctives

Independent subjunctives may also express a sense equivalent to English '**should**':

unus quisque reipublicae consulat.
'Each individual should consider the interests of the state.'

Subjunctives of this nature most commonly occur in the context of questions, when they are referred to as 'deliberative subjunctives'. These deliberative subjunctives pose questions which do not seek factual information so much as ponder aloud, often concerning a situation which seems to have no possible or satisfactory solution. Translate using either '**should**' or the patterns illustrated in '*What* **am I to** *do*?' (**present** subjunctive) or '*How* **were they to** *reply*?' (**imperfect** subjunctive):

quid dicam?
'What should I say?'/'What am I to say?'
ubi eam invenirent?
'Where should they have found her?'/'Where were they to find her?'

---

[4] *ne* + the imperative is however found occasionally in poetry and very rarely in prose.

D. Wishes or Prayers

Latin constructs wishes or prayers by using:

i) the **subjunctive on its own**;[5] or

ii) ***utinam* + subjunctive**; or

iii) (occasionally in poetry) ***ut* + subjunctive**.

ne is used where a negative is required.

A **present subjunctive** expresses a wish for the **future**:

(utinam) ille adveniat!

'**May he** come!'/'**If only he would** come!'

An **imperfect subj.** expresses a wish for the **present**:

utinam ille adesset!

'Would that he were here!'/'**If only he were** here!'

A **pluperfect subjunctive** expresses a wish for the **past**:

utinam ille advenisset!

'Would that he had come!'/'**If only he had** come!'

Observe the tense of subjunctive used and follow the formulae highlighted in bold print above.

E. Paratactical Constructions

Independent subjunctives sometimes occur beside an indicative, an imperative or a second independent subjunctive. Common examples are of the type:

cupio adsis!

(lit.) 'I wish-may you be here!', i.e. 'I hope that you will be here!'

---

[5] This method of expressing a wish is most common with wishes referring to the future.

cura valeas!

(lit.) 'Take care-be well!', i.e. 'Take care that you are well!'

fac venias!

(lit.) 'Act-you should come!', i.e. 'See to it that you come!'

velim adesses!

(lit.) 'I would like-would that you were here!', i.e. 'I wish that you were here!'

These expressions represent a colloquial form of Latin syntax, whereby two elements of speech are placed side by side with each other, i.e. in a paratactical construction (from the Greek *para* 'beside' and *taxis* 'construction'), instead of one element being subordinated to the other, as normally occurs in the written language. Since these expressions are colloquial in nature, they occur most frequently in direct speeches, letters or comedy:

id velim diligenter etiam atque etiam vobiscum et cum amicis consideretis. (Cicero, *Letters*)

lit. 'I would like-you should consider this carefully…'

i.e. 'I would like you to consider this carefully over and over again amongst yourselves and with your friends.'

Exercises for Level One

Exercise 1A[V]

The subjunctives featured in this exercise follow the same order as the descriptions given above, with some repetitions.

a) milites requiete ciboque viris reficiant!
b) huic viro dignissimo honorem reddamus!
c) ex hoc laudem sibi ne quaerant!
d) nostrum fatum ne queramur!
e) hoc in discrimine ne cunctati sitis!
f) quemadmodum haec cuncta discam?
g) defatigatus corpore animoque quemadmodum haec opera perficerem?
h) mihi cito opem ferant!
i) utinam consul tantam reipublicae operam quantam conviviis tribueret!
j) utinam ne his remediis opus fuisset!

Exercise 1B

Cicero longs to be with his wife again.

TULLIUS S.D.[6] TERENTIAE ET TULLIAE ET CICERONI SUIS.

ego minus saepe do ad vos litteras quam possum, propterea quod cum[7] omnia mihi tempora sunt misera, tum vero, cum aut scribo ad vos aut vestras lego, conficior lacrimis sic ut[8] ferre non possim...o me perditum, o adflictum! **quid** nunc **rogem** te ut[9] venias, mulierem aegram et corpore et animo confectam? non **rogem**? sine te igitur **sim**? opinor, sic agam: si est spes nostri reditus, eam **confirmes** et rem **adiuves**; sin,

---

[6] *S.D.*: i.e. *salutem dat.*

[7] *cum...tum...*: see **4. Temporal Conjunctions E** vii).

[8] *ut...possim*: see **6. Purpose and Result Clauses Part 2 A**.

[9] *ut...venias*: see **2. Indirect Speech Part 5**.

ut ego metuo, transactum est, quoquo modo potes ad me fac **venias**. unum hoc scito:[10] si te habebo, non mihi videbor plane perisse. Cicero, *Letters*

Exercise 1C

The devotion of Indian wives knows no limits.

verum **quid** ego fortissimos hoc in genere prudentiae viros **laudem**? **respiciantur** Indorum feminae quae, cum[11] more patrio complures eidem nuptae esse soleant, mortuo marito in certamen iudiciumque veniunt quam[12] ex his maxime dilexerit. victrix gaudio exultans deductaque a necessariis laetum praeferentibus vultum, coniugis se flammis superiacit et cum eo tamquam felicissima crematur. superatae cum tristitia et maerore in vita remanent. Valerius Maximus

Exercise 1D

If only the Argo had never been built!

utinam ne in nemore Pelio securibus
caesa **accidisset** abiegna ad terram trabes,
neue inde nauis incohandae[13] exordium
coepisset, quae nunc nominatur nomine
Argo, quia Argiui in ea delecti uiri
uecti petebant pellem inauratam arietis
Colchis, imperio regis Peliae, per dolum.
nam numquam era errans mea domo ecferret[14] pedem
Medea, animo aegra, amore saeuo saucia.

Ennius, *Medea Exsul*

---

[10] *scito*: the imperative, 'know…!'
[11] *cum...soleant*: see **4. Temporal Conjunctions E** v).
[12] *quam...dilexerit*: see **2. Indirect Speech Part 6**.
[13] *nauis incohandae*: see **5. Gerunds and Gerundives D** c).
[14] *ecferret pedem*: 'would carrying out her foot', i.e. 'would be leaving'.

Exercises for Level Two

Exercise 2A

a) omnia vincit Amor: et nos cedamus Amori. (Virgil)

b) quis non timeat omnia providentem et cogitantem et animadvertentem deum? (Cicero)

c) bene si amico feceris, ne pigeat fecisse. (Plautus)

d) saevas utinam exorare liceret
Eumenidas timidaeque avertere Cerberon umbrae
immemoremque tuis citius dare manibus amnem. (Statius)

e) 'moriamur, milites, et morte nostra eripiamus ex obsidione circumventas legiones.' (Livy)

f) secundis nemo confidat, adversis nemo deficiat: alternae sunt vices rerum. (Seneca)

g) cum cupieris bene laudari, quare hoc ulli debeas? ipse te lauda! (Seneca)

h) ne gaudeas vanis. (Seneca)

i) utinam [philosophi] quidem et paria dictis agerent: quid esset illis beatius? (Seneca)

j) 'prior' inquit 'ego adsum.
cur timeam dubitemve locum defendere?' (Juvenal)

Exercise 2B (i)

Let us love each other, Lesbia!

uiuamus, mea Lesbia, atque **amemus**,
rumoresque senum seueriorum
omnes unius[15] **aestimemus** assis!
soles occidere et redire possunt:
nobis cum semel occidit breuis lux,
nox est perpetua una dormienda.[16]
da mi basia mille, deinde centum,
dein mille altera, dein secunda centum,
dein usque altera mille, deinde centum.
dein, cum milia multa fecerimus,
conturbabimus illa, ne[17] sciamus,
aut ne quis malus inuidere possit,
cum tantum sciat[18] esse basiorum.

Catullus

Exercise 2B(ii)

(...and later when love is no longer reciprocated...)

miser Catulle, **desinas** ineptire,
et quod uides perisse perditum **ducas**...

Catullus

---

[15] *unius...assis*: a genitive of value, for which see the **Glossary of Technical Terms.**

[16] *dormienda*: see **5. Gerunds and Gerundives D** a).

[17] *ne...aut ne...*: see **6. Purpose and Result Clauses Part 1 B** i).

[18] *cum...sciat*: see **4. Temporal Conjunctions E** v).

Exercise 2C

Ariadne wishes Theseus had never come to Crete.

Iuppiter omnipotens, **utinam ne** tempore primo
Cnosia Cecropiae **tetigissent** litora puppes,
indomito nec dira ferens stipendia tauro
perfidus in Cretam **religasset** nauita funem,
nec malus hic celans dulci crudelia forma
consilia in nostris **requiesset** sedibus hospes!
nam **quo** me **referam**? quali spe perdita nitor?
Idaeosne **petam** montes? at gurgite lato
discernens ponti truculentum diuidit aequor.
an patris auxilium **sperem**? quemne[19] ipsa reliqui
respersum iuuenem fraterna caede secuta?
coniugis an fido **consoler** memet amore?
quine fugit lentos incuruans gurgite remos?
praeterea nullo colitur sola insula tecto,
nec patet egressus pelagi cingentibus undis.
nulla fugae ratio, nulla spes: omnia muta,
omnia sunt deserta, ostentant omnia letum.

Catullus

[19] *quemne*: '(the father) whom...?'. The same understanding must be applied to *quine* three lines below, i.e. '(the husband) who...?'.

Exercise 2D

Medea's mind is in turmoil as she contemplates killing her own children.

cor pepulit horror, membra torpescunt gelu
pectusque tremuit. ira discessit loco
materque tota coniuge expulsa redit.
egone ut[20] meorum liberum ac prolis meae
fundam cruorem? melius, a, demens furor!
incognitum istud facinus ac dirum nefas
a me quoque **absit**; quod scelus miseri luent?
scelus est Iason genitor et maius scelus
Medea mater. **occidant**, non sunt mei,
pereant. mei sunt, crimine et culpa carent,
sunt innocentes: fateor, et frater fuit.
quid, anime, titubas? ora quid lacrimae rigant
variamque nunc huc ira, nunc illuc amor
diducit? anceps aestus incertam rapit,
ut, saeva rapidi bella cum venti gerunt,
utrimque fluctus maria discordes agunt
dubiumque fervet pelagus: haut aliter meum
cor fluctuatur. ira pietatem fugat
iramque pietas-cede pietati, dolor.

Seneca, *Medea*

[20] *-ne ut,* very occasionally, as here, reinforces deliberative questions which contain no question word (i.e. questions of the type 'Am I to...?').

Exercises for Level Three

Exercise 3A

Aeneas announces games to honour the anniversary of his father's death.

'Dardanidae magni, genus alto a sanguine divum,
annuus exactis completur mensibus orbis,
ex quo reliquias divinique ossa parentis
condidimus terra maestasque sacravimus aras.
iamque dies, nisi fallor, adest, quem semper acerbum,
semper honoratum (sic di voluistis) habebo.

....

ergo agite et laetum cuncti **celebremus** honorem:
poscamus ventos, atque haec me sacra quotannis
urbe **velit** posita templis sibi ferre dicatis.
bina boum vobis Troia generatus Acestes
dat numero capita in navis; adhibete penatis
et patrios epulis et quos colit hospes Acestes.
praeterea, si nona diem mortalibus almum
Aurora extulerit radiisque retexerit orbem,
prima citae Teucris ponam certamina classis;
quique pedum cursu valet, et qui viribus audax
aut iaculo incedit melior levibusque sagittis,
seu crudo fidit pugnam committere caestu,
cuncti **adsint** meritaeque **exspectent** praemia palmae.
ore favete omnes et cingite tempora ramis.'

Virgil, *Aeneid*

Exercise 3B

Treat slaves in the same way as you would wish a master to treat you.

haec tamen praecepti mei summa est: sic cum inferiore **uiuas**, quemadmodum tecum superiorem **uelis** uiuere. quotiens in mentem uenerit quantum tibi in seruum liceat, **ueniat** in mentem tantundem in te domino tuo licere. 'at ego' inquis 'nullum habeo dominum'. bona aetas est: forsitan habebis. nescis qua aetate Hecuba seruire coeperit, qua Croesus, qua Darei mater, qua Platon, qua Diogenes? uiue cum seruo clementer, comiter quoque, et in sermonem illum admitte et in consilium et in conuictum... **colant**[21] potius te quam **timeant**. dicet aliquis nunc me uocare ad pilleum seruos et dominos de fastigio suo deicere, quod dixi '**colant** potius dominum quam **timeant**'. 'ita' inquit 'prorsus: **colant** tamquam clientes, tamquam salutatores?' hoc qui dixerit, obliuiscetur id dominis parum non esse quod deo sat est. qui colitur, et amatur: non potest amor cum timore misceri.

Seneca, *Letters*

[21] *colant*: the subject is 'slaves'.

Exercise 3C

Medea wishes that she and Jason had died, as had her brother, Absyrtus.

at non te fugiens sine me, germane, reliqui!
deficit hoc uno littera nostra loco.
quod facere ausa mea est, non audet scribere dextra.
sic ego, sed tecum, dilaceranda fui.
nec tamen extimui-quid enim post illa **timerem**?-
credere me pelago, femina iamque nocens.
numen ubi est? ubi di? meritas **subeamus**[22] in alto,
tu fraudis poenas, credulitatis ego!
compressos **utinam** Symplegades **elisissent**,
nostraque **adhaererent** ossibus ossa tuis;
aut nos Scylla rapax canibus **mersisset** edendos-
debuit ingratis Scylla nocere viris;
quaeque vomit totidem fluctus totidemque resorbet,
nos quoque Trinacriae **supposuisset** aquae!
sospes ad Haemonias victorque reverteris urbes;
ponitur ad patrios aurea lana deos.

Ovid, *Heroides*

---

[22] The subjects are Medea and Jason.

Exercises for Level Four

Exercise 4A

Milo's thoughts and feelings of bitterness as he faces the possibility of exile.

me quidem, iudices, exanimant et interimunt hae voces Milonis quas audio adsidue et quibus intersum cotidie. '**valeant**,' inquit '**valeant** cives mei; **sint** incolumes, **sint** florentes, **sint** beati; **stet** haec urbs praeclara mihique patria carissima, quoquo modo erit merita de me; tranquilla re publica mei cives, quoniam mihi cum illis non licet, sine me ipsi, sed propter me tamen **perfruantur**. ego cedam atque abibo. si mihi bona re publica frui non licuerit, at carebo mala, et quam primum tetigero bene moratam et liberam civitatem, in ea conquiescam. o frustra,' inquit 'mei suscepti labores, o spes fallaces, o cogitationes inanes meae! ego cum tribunus plebis re publica oppressa me senatui dedissem quem exstinctum acceperam, equitibus Romanis quorum vires erant debiles, bonis viris qui omnem auctoritatem Clodianis armis abiecerant, mihi umquam bonorum praesidium defuturum **putarem**? ego cum te'-mecum enim saepissime loquitur-'patriae reddidissem, mihi **putarem** in patria non futurum locum? ubi nunc senatus est quem secuti sumus, ubi equites Romani illi, illi' inquit 'tui? ubi studia municipiorum, ubi Italiae voces, ubi denique tua, M. Tulli, quae plurimis fuit auxilio, vox atque defensio? mihine ea soli qui pro te totiens morti me obtuli nihil potest opitulari?'

Cicero, *Pro Milone*

Exercise 4B

Cornutus should ask for what he wants on his birthday.

dicamus bona uerba; uenit Natalis ad aras:
quisquis ades, lingua, uir mulierque, faue.
urantur pia tura focis, **urantur** odores
quos tener e terra diuite mittit Arabs.
ipse suos Genius **adsit** uisurus honores,
cui decorent sanctas mollia serta comas.
illius puro **destillent** tempora nardo,
atque satur libo **sit madeatque** mero.

adnuat et, Cornute, tibi quodcumque rogabis.
en age, quid cessas? adnuit ille-roga.
auguror: uxoris fidos optabis amores;
iam reor hoc ipsos edidicisse deos.
nec tibi malueris totum quaecumque per orbem
fortis arat ualido rusticus arua boue,
nec tibi gemmarum quicquid felicibus Indis
nascitur, Eoi qua maris unda rubet.

uota cadunt.[23] uiden ut strepitantibus aduolet alis
flauaque coniugio uincula portet Amor?
uincula quae maneant semper, dum tarda senectus
inducat rugas inficiatque comas.
eueniat, Natalis, auis prolemque **ministret**,
ludat et ante tuos turba nouella pedes.

Tibullus, *Elegies*

[23] *cadunt*: here 'are successful'.

Exercise 4C

Ovid decides to 'change his tune'.

verba mihi desunt eadem tam saepe roganti,
    iamque pudet vanas fine carere preces.
taedia consimili fieri de carmine vobis,
    quidque petam cunctos edidicisse reor.
nostraque quid portet iam nostis epistula, quamvis
    cera sit a vinclis non labefacta meis.
ergo **mutetur** scripti sententia nostri,
    ne totiens contra, quam rapit amnis, eam.
quod bene de vobis speravi, ignoscite, amici:
    talia peccandi iam mihi finis erit.
nec gravis uxori **dicar**: quae scilicet in me
    quam proba tam timida est experiensque parum.
hoc quoque, Naso, feres: etenim peiora tulisti.
    iam tibi sentiri sarcina nulla potest.
ductus ab armento taurus **detrectet** aratrum,
    subtrahat et duro colla novella iugo.
nos, quibus adsuevit fatum crudeliter uti,
    ad mala iam pridem non sumus ulla rudes.
venimus in Geticos fines: **moriamur** in illis,
    Parcaque ad extremum qua mea coepit **eat**.

Ovid, *Epistulae ex Ponto*

Exercises for Level Five

Exercise 5A

Horace cannot give up writing his kind of poetry.

sunt quibus in satira videar nimis acer et ultra
legem tendere opus; sine nervis altera quidquid
composui pars esse putat, similisque meorum
mille die versus deduci posse. Trebati,
quid faciam praescribe. 'quiescas.' ne faciam, inquis,
omnino versus? 'aio.' peream male si non
optimum erat: verum nequeo dormire. 'ter uncti
transnanto Tiberim somno quibus est opus alto,
irriguumque mero sub noctem corpus habento.
aut si tantus amor scribendi te rapit, aude
Caesaris invicti res dicere, multa laborum
praemia laturus.' cupidum, pater optime, vires
deficiunt: neque enim quivis horrentia pilis
agmina nec fracta pereuntis cuspide Gallos
aut labentis equo describat vulnera Parthi.
'attamen et iustum poteras et scribere fortem,
Scipiadam ut sapiens Lucilius.' haud mihi deero
cum res ipsa feret: nisi dextro tempore, Flacci
verba per attentam non ibunt Caesaris aurem,
cui male si palpere recalcitrat undique tutus.
'quanto rectius hoc quam tristi laedere versu
Pantolabum scurram Nomentanumque nepotem,
cum sibi quisque timet, quamquam est intactus, et odit!'
quid faciam? saltat Milonius, ut semel icto
accessit fervor capiti numerusque lucernis;
Castor gaudet equis, ovo prognatus eodem
pugnis; quot capitum vivunt, totidem studiorum
milia: me pedibus delectat claudere verba
Lucili ritu nostrum melioris utroque. Horace, *Satires*

Exercise 5B

The present danger is very close to home.

'itaque uos ego, milites, non eo solum animo quo aduersus alios hostes soletis, pugnare uelim, sed cum indignatione quadam atque ira, uelut si seruos uideatis uestros arma repente contra uos ferentes. licuit ad Erycem clausos ultimo supplicio humanorum, fame interficere; licuit uictricem classem in Africam traicere atque intra paucos dies sine ullo certamine Carthaginem delere; ueniam dedimus precantibus, emisimus ex obsidione, pacem cum uictis fecimus, tutelae deinde nostrae duximus, cum Africo bello urgerentur. pro his impertitis furiosum iuuenem sequentes oppugnatum[24] patriam nostram ueniunt. atque utinam pro decore tantum hoc uobis et non pro salute esset certamen! non de possessione Siciliae ac Sardiniae, de quibus quondam agebatur, sed pro Italia uobis est pugnandum. nec est alius ab tergo exercitus qui, nisi nos uincimus, hosti obsistat, nec Alpes aliae sunt, quas dum superant, comparari noua possint praesidia; hic est obstandum, milites, uelut si ante Romana moenia pugnemus. unusquisque se non corpus suum sed coniugem ac liberos paruos armis protegere putet; nec domesticas solum agitet curas sed identidem hoc animo reputet nostras nunc intueri manus senatum populumque Romanum: qualis nostra uis uirtusque fuerit, talem deinde fortunam illius urbis ac Romani imperii fore.'

Livy

---

[24] *oppugnatum*: the supine, for which see the **Glossary of Technical Terms**.

Exercise 5C

A rallying cry for the imminent Parthian campaign.

arma deus Caesar dites meditatur ad Indos,
    et freta gemmiferi findere classe maris.
magna, viri, merces: parat ultima terra triumphos,
    Thybris, et Euphrates sub tua iura fluet;
sera, sed Ausoniis veniet provincia virgis;
    assuescent Latio Partha tropaea Iovi.
ite agite, expertae bello date lintea prorae,
    et solitum armigeri ducite munus equi!
omina fausta cano. Crassos cladem que piate!
    ite et Romanae consulite historiae!
Mars pater, et sacrae fatalia lumina Vestae,
    ante meos obitus sit precor illa dies,
qua videam spoliis oneratos Caesaris axes,
    ad vulgi plausus saepe resistere equos,
inque sinu carae nixus spectare puellae
    incipiam et titulis oppida capta legam,
tela fugacis equi et bracati militis arcus,
    et subter captos arma sedere duces!
ipsa tuam serva prolem, Venus: hoc sit in aevum,
    cernis ab Aenea quod superesse caput.
praeda sit haec illis, quorum meruere labores:
    mi sat erit Sacra plaudere posse Via.

Propertius, *Elegies*

Chapter 9

CONDITIONAL SENTENCES

> Parallel Revision: Imperfect & Pluperfect Subjunctives, Kennedy 115-25, 133-41, *CLG* 7d-e, 8b, 9.2, *OLG* pp. 37-60.

A. What are Conditional Sentences?

Conditional sentences are those which contain a condition, i.e. a clause introduced in English by 'If...' or 'Unless...':

> '*If* it is too hot in early summer, the harvest is poor.'
> '*Unless* you leave early, you will not arrive in time.'
> '*If* Marcus had arrived on time, he would have been able to attend the meeting.'

The part of the sentence which expresses the condition (i.e. the part introduced by 'If /Unless...') is called the **protasis**. The other part of the sentence is called the **apodosis**. Most commonly the protasis precedes the apodosis in a sentence, but the reverse order is also occasionally found.

If the protasis is positive (i.e. contains no negative words such as 'not', 'never', 'nowhere' etc.), it is usually introduced in Latin by *si*; if the protasis contains a negative word, it is usually introduced by *nisi* in place of *si*;[1] so, instead of *si... numquam*, Latin usually writes *nisi...umquam*; for this reason, it is often better to translate *nisi* as 'If...not/nothing/never etc.' rather than 'Unless'.

---

[1] Where the negative applies only to one particular word, *si...non...* is used:
si hoc non semel sed bis accidit...
'If this happens **not** once but twice...'.

Double conditions, i.e. 'If x happens or y happens' or 'Whether x happens or y happens', are introduced either by *sive...sive* or by *seu...seu*:

sive legit sive dormit, ad eum adire non audeo.
'If he is reading or if he is sleeping/Whether he is reading or sleeping, I do not dare to approach him.'

After *si*, *quis/quid* etc. means 'anyone/anything' etc.

si quem agnovisti, nomen praetoribus defer!
'If you recognised anyone, report his name to the praetors!'

'But if...' in Latin is expressed by *sin* or *quod si*.

There are two main categories of conditional sentences, those which contain conditions said to be **real** and those which contain conditions said to be **unreal**.

B. Real Conditions

Real conditions are those where the condition and its consequence are regarded as actual or true:

'If my opponent is weak, I will easily beat him.'
'If it rains too hard, rivers overflow.'

These conditions are expressed by the **indicative** mood:

si vales, bene est.
'If you are well, it is good.'
si cras venies, tibi pecuniam dare potero.
'If you come (lit. 'will come') tomorrow, I will be able to give you the money.'

C. Unreal Conditions

Unreal conditions are those where the condition and its consequence are regarded as **hypothetical** or **unreal**:

'If he were to discover the ruins of that city, we would all learn more about the past.'

'If they had told the truth, they would not have got into trouble.'

To express such conditions, Latin uses the **subjunctive** mood in both the protasis and the apodosis. These unreal conditions may refer to the future (vague future conditions), the present (present unfulfilled or unreal conditions) or the past (past unfulfilled or unreal conditions).

i) **Vague Future Conditions** are conditions which refer to the consequences of a hypothetical possibility in the future:

'If he were to marry that woman, he would dishonour his own family.'

'If the temple were to collapse, it would be a sacrilege.'

The **present subjunctive** is used in both the protasis and the apodosis:

si me videant, mihi gratias agant.

'If they were to see me, they would thank me.'

si dives fiam, te adiuvem.

'If I were to become rich, I would help you.'

As these examples demonstrate, translate vague future conditions using the formula:

'**If x were to happen, y would result.**'

ii) **Present Unreal or Unfulfilled Conditions** refer to situations in the present which are not actually true or fulfilled:

'If the taxes were fair (clearly they are *not* perceived to be fair), people would not mind paying them (clearly people *do* mind paying them).'

'If the Romans had the upper hand (apparently they do *not*), they would not be suffering so many casualties (which they *are* in fact suffering).'

Present unfulfilled or unreal conditions are expressed by using the **imperfect subjunctive** in both the protasis and the apodosis:

nisi ratis hieme gravissima tunderetur, nautae ad litora facillime appellerent.

'If the ship were not being buffeted by such a severe storm, the sailors would easily be reaching the shore.'

si hoc facere possem, statim facerem.

'If I were able to do this, I would be doing it immediately.'

As these examples illustrate, translate these present unreal conditions using the formula:

'**If x were happening, y would result/be resulting.**'

iii) **Past Unreal or Unfulfilled Conditions** refer to the past and describe the consequences of situations which might have happened but did not:

'If the centurion had found out about it (clearly he had *not*), you would certainly have been punished (but you were *not* punished).'

'If he had not contracted the disease (but he *had*), he would not have died (which he *did).*'

Latin uses the **pluperfect subjunctive** to express such conditions:

nisi librum amisissem, rationem discere potuissem.

'If I had not lost the book, I would have been able to learn the system.'

si auxilium ab eis petiissemus, libenter dedissent.

'If we had sought help from them, they would have given it gladly.'

So, translate past unreal conditions using the formula:

'**If x had happened, y would have resulted.**'

D. Summary of Unreal Conditions

As illustrated above, the key to translating unreal conditions lies in observing the *tense* of the subjunctive in both protasis and apodosis. Then use the following formulae:

Tense of Subjunctive	**English Formula**
Present (in both parts)	'If x were to happen, y would result.'
Imperfect (in both parts)	'If x were happening, y would be resulting.'
Pluperfect (in both parts)	'If x had happened, y would have resulted.'

E. Mixed Conditions

i) Sometimes, a writer may want to formulate a conditional sentence where the protasis and apodosis refer to different spheres of time:

> 'If he had not died (past unreal), he would be an excellent general now (present unreal).'

In this situation, Latin uses the tense of the subjunctive appropriate to the type of condition which the protasis and the apodosis individually represent:

> *nisi ille mortuus esset* (**pluperfect**), *iam imperator optimus esset* (**imperfect**).

ii) Very occasionally, conditions are mixed by using an indicative in one clause and a subjunctive in the other. The intention therefore is to express one part of the sentence as unreal and the other as real:[2]

---

[2] This does not apply if the subjunctive occurs in the apodosis and is a jussive subjunctive [see **8. Independent Subjunctives B** i)]:

> *si hoc verum est, gaudeamus!*
> 'If this is true, let us be glad!'

si id verum esset, stultus sum.

'If that were the truth (**unreal**), I am a fool (**real**).'

The full effect of this statement relies on the speaker's confidence that no-one actually considers him a fool. Since the speaker reckons that no-one does believe him to be a fool, ironically the use of the indicative in the apodosis gives added weight to the unreal status of the protasis: by constructing his utterance in this way the speaker implies 'I am not a fool; therefore, that is very definitely *not* the truth.'

F. Elliptical Conditions

Sometimes the protasis of a conditional sentence is not actually expressed but is left to be inferred from common knowledge or from the surrounding context:

magnitudinem equi miratus esses!

'You would have marvelled at the size of the horse (understand: "if you had seen it").'

Elsewhere the protasis of a conditional statement is expressed only allusively, using, for example, an ablative absolute instead of a *si*-clause:

Cicerone patrono, causam non perdidissemus.

'If Cicero had been our counsel (lit. Cicero being our counsel), we would not have lost our case.'

The tense of the subjunctive used in the 'apodosis' of these elliptical conditions is usually an accurate guide to translating the suppressed or allusively expressed 'protasis'. So, for example, if the subjunctive is present, follow the rules for vague future conditions etc.

Exercises for Level One

Exercise 1A

The content of these sentences follows the same order as the descriptions given above, with some repetitions.

a) si sero egrediemini, sero pervenietis.
b) si in latrones incidamus, haud facile nos defendamus.
c) nisi istam amicam umquam videas, miserrimusne sis?
d) si reus mentiretur, nonne culpam in vultu eius videremus?
e) si tecum iter facere vellem, ita facerem.
f) nisi doctrinam nostram neglexisses, optimam vitae rationem invenisses.
g) si uxores viris persuadere conatae essent, ita potuissent.
h) nisi exercitus noster magnis itineribus defatigatus esset, iam manum superiorem consequeretur.
i) si tu pauper esses, ego omnium pauperrimus sum!
j) hostibus a porta praetoria repulsis, illac castra effugere possimus.

Exercise 1B

Nothing is more inept than an inept smile.

Egnatius, quod candidos habet dentes,
renidet usque quaque. **si** ad rei **uentum est**
subsellium, cum orator excitat fletum,
renidet ille; **si** ad pii rogum fili
lugetur, orba cum flet unicum mater,
renidet ille. quidquid est, ubicumque est,
quodcumque agit, renidet: hunc habet morbum,
neque elegantem, ut arbitror, neque urbanum.
quare monendum[3] est te mihi, bone Egnati.
si urbanus **esses** aut Sabinus aut Tiburs
aut pinguis Vmber aut obesus Etruscus
aut Lanuuinus ater atque dentatus
aut Transpadanus, ut[4] meos quoque attingam,
aut quilubet, qui puriter lauit dentes,
tamen renidere usque quaque te **nollem**:
nam risu inepto res ineptior nulla est.

Catullus

---

[3] *monendum...*: see **5. Gerunds and Gerundives D** a).
[4] *ut...attingam*: see **6. Purpose and Result Clauses Part 1 B** ii).

Exercise 1C

Quinctius is ashamed that the Aequi and Volsci were able to reach the walls of Rome with impunity in his consulship.

['Although I do not feel any guilt for my part, however I have come into your presence with great shame. To think that you know-and that it will be handed down to posterity-that the Aequi and Volsci came in arms to the walls of Rome with impunity, when I, T. Quinctius, was consul for the fourth time!...]

hanc[5] ego ignominiam...**si** huic potissimum imminere anno **scissem**, uel exsilio uel morte, **si** alia fuga honoris non **esset**, **uitassem**. ergo **si** uiri arma illa **habuissent** quae in portis fuere nostris, capi Roma me consule **potuit**? satis honorum, satis superque uitae erat; mori consulem tertium oportuit. quem tandem ignauissimi hostium contempsere? nos consules an uos Quirites? **si** culpa in nobis **est**, **auferte** imperium indignis et, **si** id parum **est**, insuper poenas **expetite**: **si** in uobis[6], nemo deorum nec hominum **sit**[7], qui[8] uestra puniat peccata, Quirites: uosmet tantum eorum paeniteat...'

Livy

Students working at Level One should now attempt the Revision Exercises in Chapter 12.

---

[5] *hanc ego ignominiam* etc.: i.e. *si scissem hanc ignominiam huic potissimum anno imminere*; see **2. Indirect Speeech Part 2**. *hanc ego ignominiam* is brought forward for emphasis.

[6] *si in uobis*, i.e. *si in uobis culpa est.*

[7] *sit...paeniteat*: see **8. Independent Subjunctives B** i) and footnote 2 in this chapter above.

[8] *qui...puniat*: see **6. Purpose and Result Clauses Part 2 B**.

Exercises for Level Two

Exercise 2A

a) 'sceleratus et nefarius fueris, si quicquam misericordia adductus feceris.' (Saying quoted by Cicero)

b) nulla est igitur excusatio peccati, si amici causa peccaveris. (Cicero)

c) o quam contempta res est homo, nisi supra humana surrexerit! (Seneca)

d) nolite existimare, maiores nostros armis rempublicam ex parva magnam fecisse. si ita res esset, multo pulcherrimam eam nos haberemus. (Sallust)

e) quod si regum atque imperatorum animi virtus in pace ita uti in bello valeret, aequabilius atque constantius sese res humanae haberent, neque aliud alio ferri neque mutari ac misceri omnia cerneres. (Sallust)

f) si quid haberem quod ad te scriberem, facerem id et pluribus verbis et saepius. (Cicero)

g) si saperem, doctas odissem iure sorores[9],
numina cultori perniciosa suo. (Ovid)

h) vitaret caelum Phaethon, si viveret, et quos
optarat stulte, tangere nollet equos. (Ovid)

i) sed tacitus pasci si posset corvus, haberet
plus dapis et rixae multo minus invidiaeque. (Horace)

j) vivere si recte nescis, decede peritis. (Horace)

[9] *doctas...sorores*: i.e. the Muses.

Exercise 2B

Dido rebukes and pleads with Aeneas.

'dissimulare etiam sperasti, perfide, tantum
posse nefas tacitusque mea decedere terra?
nec te noster amor nec te data dextera quondam
nec moritura tenet crudeli funere Dido?
quin etiam[10] hiberno moliris sidere classem
et mediis properas Aquilonibus ire per altum,
crudelis? quid, **si** non arva aliena domosque
ignotas **peteres**, et Troia antiqua **maneret**,
Troia per undosum **peteretur** classibus aequor?
mene fugis? per ego has lacrimas dextramque tuam te
(quando aliud mihi iam miserae nihil ipsa reliqui),
per conubia nostra, per inceptos hymenaeos,
si bene quid de te **merui**, **fuit** aut tibi quicquam
dulce meum, miserere domus labentis et istam,
oro, **si** quis adhuc precibus locus, exue mentem.

[On account of you I have incurred hatred; on account of you my honour and reputation are no more. For whom or what are you abandoning me? Why do I delay? Or is it until my brother should destroy my city or Iarbas should lead me off into captivity?]

saltem **si** qua mihi de te suscepta **fuisset**
ante fugam suboles, **si** quis mihi parvulus aula
luderet Aeneas, qui te tamen ore referret[11],
non equidem omnino capta ac deserta **viderer**.'

Virgil, *Aeneid*

---

[10] See **7. Verbs of Fearing/*quominus* & *quin* Part 2 C**.
[11] *qui...referret*: see **6. Purpose and Result Clauses Part 2 B**.

Exercise 2C

Manlius Torquatus argues that the Roman prisoners lack spirit.

[After defeat at the battle of Cannae, the remnant of Roman troops returned to their camps (from which some soon escaped). Two days later, about 8,000 men surrendered to Hannibal, on the condition that they would be freed on the payment of a ransom. Representatives of these prisoners were sent to Rome to plead their cause. They argued that the squalor and degradation they were suffering and the bodies of the dead would move the senate to pity. Torquatus opened the debate in the senate. He felt that the envoys had almost boasted about their surrender and that the situation might provide a dangerous precedent for military discipline. He reminded the envoys that Sempronius Tuditanus had tried to lead a sally out of the camp under the cover and safety of darkness…]

si, ut[12] auorum memoria P. Decius tribunus militum in Samnio, **si**, ut nobis adulescentibus priore Punico bello Calpurnius Flamma trecentis uoluntariis, cum[13] ad tumulum eos capiendum[14] situm inter medios duceret hostes, dixit "moriamur[15], milites, et morte nostra eripiamus ex obsidione circumuentas legiones"-**si** hoc P. Sempronius **diceret**, nec uiros quidem nec Romanos uos **duceret**, **si** nemo tantae uirtutis **exstitisset** comes. uiam non ad gloriam magis quam ad salutem ferentem demonstrat; reduces in patriam ad parentes, ad coniuges ac liberos facit. ut[16] seruemini, deest uobis animus: quid, **si** moriendum[17] pro patria **esset**, **faceretis**? quinquaginta milia ciuium sociorumque circa uos eo ipso die caesa iacent. **si** tot exempla uirtutis non **mouent**, nihil unquam **mouebit**; **si** tanta clades uilem uitam non **fecit**, nulla **faciet**...' Livy

---

[12] *ut...ut...*: here 'as...as...'.

[13] *cum...duceret*: see **4. Temporal Conjunctions E** vi).

[14] *ad tumulum...capiendum*: see **5. Gerunds and Gerundives D** b) iii).

[15] *moriamur...eripiamus*: see **8. Independent Subjunctives B** i).

[16] *ut seruemini*: see **6. Purpose and Result Clauses Part 1 B** i).

[17] *moriendum*: see **5. Gerunds and Gerundives D** a).

Exercises for Level Three

Exercise 3A

Cicero ponders what Cato might be like if he had followed a different school of thought.

Nostri autem illi (fatebor enim, Cato, me quoque in adulescentia diffisum ingenio meo quaesisse adiumenta doctrinae), nostri, inquam, illi a[18] Platone et Aristotele, moderati homines et temperati, aiunt apud sapientem valere aliquando gratiam; viri boni[19] esse misereri; distincta genera esse delictorum et dispares poenas; esse apud hominem constantem ignoscendi locum; ipsum sapientem saepe aliquid opinari, quod nesciat; irasci nonnumquam; exorari eundem et placari; quod dixerit, interdum, **si** ita rectius **sit**, mutare; de sententia decedere aliquando; omnes virtutes mediocritate quadam esse moderatas. hos ad magistros **si** qua te fortuna, Cato, cum ista natura **detulisset**, non tu quidem vir melior **esses** nec fortior nec temperantior nec iustior (neque enim esse potes), sed paulo ad lenitatem propensior. non **accusares** nullis adductus inimicitiis, nulla lacessitus iniuria, pudentissimum hominem, summa dignitate atque honestate praeditum; **putares**, cum in eiusdem anni custodia te atque L. Murenam fortuna posuisset, aliquo te cum hoc rei publicae vinculo esse coniunctum; quod atrociter in senatu dixisti, aut non **dixisses** aut, **si posuisses**, mitiorem in partem **interpretarere**. ac te ipsum, quantum ego opinione auguror, nunc et animi quodam impetu concitatum et vi naturae atque ingenii elatum et recentibus praeceptorum studiis flagrantem iam usus flectet, dies leniet, aetas mitigabit.

Cicero, *Pro Murena*

---

[18] *a*: translate here 'following'.

[19] *viri boni*: genitive of characteristic, for which see the **Glossary of Technical Terms**.

Exercise 3B

Ovid recommends his guidance to lovers.

ad mea, decepti iuuenes, praecepta uenite,
quos suus ex omni parte fefellit amor.
discite sanari per quem didicistis amare;
una manus uobis uulnus opemque feret.
terra salutares herbas eademque nocentes
nutrit, et urticae proxima saepe rosa est;
uulnus in Herculeo quae quondam fecerat hoste,
uulneris auxilium Pelias hasta tulit.
(sed, quaecunque uiris, uobis quoque dicta, puellae,
credite: diuersis partibus arma damus.
e quibus ad uestros **si** quid non **pertinet** usus,
at tamen exemplo multa docere potest.)
utile propositum est saeuas extinguere flammas
nec seruum uitii pectus habere sui.
uixisset Phyllis, **si** me **foret usa** magistro,
et per quod nouies, saepius **isset** iter.
nec moriens Dido summa **uidisset** ab arce
Dardanias uento uela dedisse rates,
nec dolor **armasset** contra sua uiscera matrem,
quae socii damno sanguinis ulta uirum est.
arte mea Tereus, quamuis Philomela placeret,
per facinus fieri non **meruisset** auis.
da mihi Pasiphaen, iam tauri ponet amorem;
da Phaedram, Phaedrae turpis abibit amor.
redde Parin nobis, Helenen Menelaus habebit
nec manibus Danais Pergama uicta cadent.
impia **si** nostros **legisset** Scylla libellos,
haesisset capiti purpura, Nise, tuo.
me duce damnosas, homines, conpescite curas,
rectaque cum sociis me duce nauis eat.

Ovid, *Remedia Amoris*

Exercises for Level Four

Exercise 4A

Philosophy alone can cure restlessness of mind.

si possent homines, proinde ac sentire videntur
pondus inesse animo quod se gravitate fatiget,
e quibus id fiat causis quoque noscere et unde
tanta mali tamquam moles in pectore constet,
haud ita vitam **agerent** ut nunc plerumque videmus
quid sibi quisque velit nescire et quaerere semper
commutare locum quasi onus deponere possit.
exit saepe foras magnis ex aedibus ille,
esse domi quem pertaesumst, subitoque revertit,
quippe foris nilo melius qui sentiat esse.
currit agens mannos ad villam praecipitanter,
auxilium tectis quasi ferre ardentibus instans;
oscitat extemplo, tetigit cum limina villae,
aut abit in somnum gravis atque oblivia quaerit,
aut etiam properans urbem petit atque revisit.
hoc se quisque modo fugit, at quem scilicet, ut fit,
effugere haud potis est, ingratis haeret et odit
propterea, morbi quia causam non tenet aeger;
quam bene **si videat**, iam rebus quisque relictis
naturam primum **studeat** cognoscere rerum,
temporis aeterni quoniam, non unius horae,
ambigitur status, in quo sit mortalibus omnis
aetas, post mortem quae restat cumque manenda.

Lucretius, *De Rerum Natura*

Exercise 4B

Gallus is lovesick.

omnes 'unde amor iste' rogant 'tibi?' venit Apollo,
'Galle, quid insanis?' inquit 'tua cura Lycoris
perque nives alium perque horrida castra secuta est.'
venit et agresti capitis Silvanus honore,
florentis ferulas et grandia lilia quassans.
Pan deus Arcadiae venit, quem vidimus ipsi
sanguineis ebuli bacis minioque rubentem.
'ecquis erit modus?' inquit 'Amor non talia curat,
nec lacrimis crudelis Amor nec gramina rivis
nec cytiso saturantur apes nec fronde capellae.'
tristis at ille 'tamen cantabitis, Arcades' inquit
'montibus haec vestris, soli cantare periti
Arcades. o mihi tum quam molliter ossa **quiescant**,
vestra meos olim **si** fistula **dicat** amores!
atque utinam ex vobis unus vestrique fuissem
aut custos gregis aut maturae vinitor uvae!
certe **sive** mihi Phyllis **sive esset** Amyntas,
seu quicumque furor (quid tum, **si** fuscus Amyntas?
et nigrae violae sunt et vaccinia nigra),
mecum inter salices lenta sub vite **iaceret**;
serta mihi Phyllis **legeret**, **cantaret** Amyntas.
hic gelidi fontes, hic mollia prata, Lycori,
hic nemus; hic ipso tecum **consumerer** aevo.
nunc insanus amor duri me Martis in armis
tela inter media atque adversos detinet hostis.

Virgil, *Eclogues*

Exercises for Level Five

Exercise 5A

Four poems by Martial explicitly or implicitly flattering Domitian.

i) Alcide, Latio nunc agnoscende Tonanti,
postquam pulchra dei Caesaris ora geris,
si tibi tunc isti uultus habitusque fuissent,
cesserunt manibus cum fera monstra tuis,
Argolico famulum non te seruire tyranno
uidissent gentes saeuaque regna pati;
sed tu iussisses Eurysthea: nec tibi fallax
portasset Nessi perfida dona Lichas;
Oetaei sine lege rogi securus adisses
astra patris summi, quae tibi poena dedit;
Lydia nec dominae traxisses pensa superbae
nec Styga uidisses Tartareumque canem.
nunc tibi Iuno fauet, nunc te tua diligit Hebe;
nunc te si uideat Nympha, remittet Hylan!

ii) si quid forte petam timido gracilique libello,
inproba non fuerit si mea charta, dato.
et si non dederis, Caesar, permitte rogari:
offendunt numquam tura precesque Iouem.
qui fingit sacros auro uel marmore uultus,
non facit ille deos: qui rogat, ille facit.

iii) ad cenam si me diuersa uocaret in astra
hinc inuitator Caesaris, inde Iouis,
astra licet propius, Palatia longius essent,
responsa ad superos haec referenda darem:
'Quaerite qui malit fieri conuiua Tonantis:
me meus in terris Iuppiter ecce tenet.'

iv) si desiderium, Caesar, populique patrumque
respicis et Latiae gaudia uera togae,
redde deum uotis poscentibus. inuidet hosti
Roma suo, ueniat laurea multa licet:
terrarum dominum propius uidet ille tuoque
terretur uultu barbarus et fruitur.

Martial

Exercise 5B

Scylla's soliloquy on observing Minos from the walls.

utque sedebat
candida Dictaei spectans tentoria regis,
'laeter' ait 'doleamne geri lacrimabile bellum
in dubio est: doleo quod Minos hostis amanti est,
sed, nisi bella forent, numquam mihi cognitus esset.
me tamen accepta poterat deponere bellum
obside: me comitem, me pacis pignus haberet.
si quae te peperit talis, pulcherrime regum,
qualis es ipse fuit, merito deus arsit in illa.
o ego ter felix, si pennis lapsa per auras
Cnosiaci possem castris insistere regis,
fassaque me flammasque meas, qua dote, rogarem,
vellet emi; tantum patrias ne posceret arces!
nam pereant potius sperata cubilia, quam sim
proditione potens-quamvis saepe utile vinci
victoris placidi fecit clementia multis.
iusta gerit certe pro nato bella perempto,
et causaque valet causamque tenentibus armis.
at, puto, vincemur: qui si manet exitus urbem,
cur suus haec illi reseret mea moenia Mavors
et non noster amor? melius sine caede moraque
impensaque sui poterit superare cruoris.
....
coepta placent, et stat sententia tradere mecum
dotalem patriam finemque imponere bello;
....
altera iamdudum succensa cupidine tanto
perdere gauderet, quodcumque obstaret amori.
et cur ulla foret me fortior? ire per ignes
et gladios ausim; nec in hoc tamen ignibus ullis
aut gladiis opus est, opus est mihi crine paterno.
illa mihi est auro pretiosior, illa beatam
purpura me votique mei factura potentem.' Ovid, *Met.*

Exercise 5C

Why do you resent death?

denique si vocem rerum natura repente
mittat et hoc alicui nostrum sic increpet ipsa
'quid tibi tanto operest, mortalis, quod nimis aegris
luctibus indulges? quid mortem congemis ac fles?
nam si grata fuit tibi vita anteacta priorque
et non omnia pertusum congesta quasi in vas
commoda perfluxere atque ingrata interiere,
cur non ut plenus vitae conviva recedis
aequo animoque capis securam, stulte, quietem?
sin ea quae fructus cumque es periere profusa
vitaque in offensast, cur amplius addere quaeris,
rursum quod pereat male et ingratum occidat omne,
non potius vitae finem facis atque laboris?
nam tibi praeterea quod machiner inveniamque,
quod placeat, nil est: eadem sunt omnia semper.
si tibi non annis corpus iam marcet et artus
confecti languent, eadem tamen omnia restant,
omnia si pergas vivendo vincere saecla,
atque etiam potius, si numquam sis moriturus',
quid respondemus, nisi iustam intendere litem
naturam et veram verbis exponere causam?
grandior hic vero si iam seniorque queratur
atque obitum lamentetur miser amplius aequo,
non merito inclamet magis et voce increpet acri?
'aufer abhinc lacrimas, balatro, et compesce querelas.
omnia perfunctus vitai praemia marces.
sed quia semper aves quod abest, praesentia temnis,
imperfecta tibi elapsast ingrataque vita
et nec opinanti mors ad caput adstitit ante
quam satur ac plenus possis discedere rerum.
nunc aliena tua tamen aetate omnia mitte
aequo animoque agedum gnatis concede: necessest.'
iure, ut opinor, agat, iure increpet inciletque. Lucretius

Chapter 10

COPING WITH *QUI, QUAE, QUOD*, etc.[1]

Parallel Revision: Forms of Relative & Interrogative Pronouns, Kennedy 97-8, *CLG* 5.7, 5.9, *OLG* pp. 27-8.

A. The scope of this chapter

The main aim of this chapter is to provide help with encountering *qui, quae, quod* etc. in all of the contexts in which these forms occur. Some of these contexts have already been met: the basic usage of the relative pronoun was described in the first chapter, on **Relative Clauses**, and the sixth chapter, on **Purpose and Result Clauses**, revealed three further types of clauses which this pronoun introduces. The current chapter provides a quick overview of these functions of the relative pronoun and then completes the picture by introducing three more.

It is not only the relative pronoun, however, that has the forms *qui, quae, quod* etc. In fact, the forms of the relative pronoun overlap with most or all of the forms of:

i) *quis, quis, quid?*, 'Who...?'/'What...?' etc., i.e. the interrogative pronoun, which introduces direct and indirect questions;

ii) *qui, quae, quod?*, 'Which (*noun*)...?', i.e. the interrogative adjective, which also introduces questions;[2]

iii) *quis, qua, quid* and *qui, quae, quod*, the indefinite pronoun and adjective respectively, which occur after *si* (or *seu/sive*), *nisi*, *num* and *ne* (or *neu/neve*) and mean 'anyone'/'anything' or 'any' respectively.

---

[1] Chapters 10 & 11 intended for those working at Level Two and above.

[2] For the forms and functions of these words see Kennedy 97-8, *CLG* 7 & 9 or *OLG* p. 28 and the **Glossary of Technical Terms**.

Since this overlap in forms is in itself a potential cause of difficulty and since the intention of this chapter is to provide help with **encountering** *qui, quae, quod* etc. in a text, this chapter also covers certain uses of the interrogative pronoun, as part of the final section describing those uses of *qui*, *quae, quod* etc. which occur in fixed forms in specific contexts.[3]

B. Coping with the relative pronoun: the first step

A clause introduced by the relative pronoun contains either an indicative or a subjunctive verb. Since the sense or function of this clause is affected by this choice of mood (i.e. indicative or subjunctive), it is critical to establish the mood of the verb before attempting to translate.

C. The relative pronoun with the indicative

A relative clause containing an indicative verb is, so to speak, an 'ordinary' relative clause. The function of these ordinary relative clauses is to *describe*, or, in the case of 'connecting' relatives, *replace* the antecedent, as outlined in more detail in the first chapter, **Relative Clauses**.

D. The relative pronoun with the subjunctive[4]

The earlier chapters describe three uses of the relative pronoun with the subjunctive, as summarized in the following table, the right hand column of which indicates the location of the full description:

[3] There are no specific uses of the indefinite pronoun which cause difficulty.

[4] For the interrogative pronoun with the subjunctive, see **8. Independent Subjunctives C**.

	Type of Clause	**Translate**	**Chapter**
i)	Subordinate clause in indirect speech	(as though an indicative)	**2. Part 4 E**
ii)	Purpose	'who was/were to...'	**6. Part 1 C**
iii)	Result	'(of the sort) who...'	**6. Part 2 B**

Three more uses may be added:

iv) occasionally, *qui* + subjunctive suggests **a reason** for a situation or event. In this sense *qui* is sometimes strengthened by a preceding *quippe*, *utpote* or *ut*. Translate either '**inasmuch as he/she/it** etc.' or '**since**' etc.:

> *aquila, quae ungulas multas et acres habeat, apta ad praedam rapiendam est.*
> 'The eagle, *inasmuch as/since* it has many sharp talons, is well adapted to seizing prey.'

When a relative pronoun is used with the subjunctive to achieve this subtlety of meaning, the descriptive function of the relative clause nevertheless remains strong. So, the above relative clause *describes* the eagle as much as it explains *why* it is well adapted to seizing prey.

v) in addition to suggesting *why* something happens, the subjunctive after a relative pronoun can also suggest the sense of '**although**':

> *feles, quae celerrime currere possit, saepe tamen totum diem dormire mavult.*
> 'The cat, *although* it can run very fast, often, however, prefers to sleep all day long.'

The descriptive function of the relative clause again remains strong when the relative pronoun is used in this sense. So, the above relative clause *describes* the cat's ability to run very fast. This usage of *qui* is very rare.

vi) a subjunctive may occur after a relative pronoun or a 'connecting relative', when the clause expresses the **apodosis** of an **unreal condition** (see **9. Conditional Sentences C**):

> *Caelius vir summa astutia erat, qui tamen condemnatus esset, nisi a Cicerone defensus esset.*
> 'Caelius was a man of great astuteness, who would have been condemned, however, if he had not been defended by Cicero.'

E. Specific uses of relative/interrogative pronouns[5]

The following specific uses of relative and interrogative pronouns are organized in the manner in which they will be encountered in texts, i.e. according to the specific forms themselves (respectively *quam*, *quod*, *quo*, *qua* & *qui*), rather than under the separate categories of relative and interrogative pronouns.

a) **quam** occurs in seven main usages, each specific to a context. The key to translating *quam*, therefore, is to establish in which context the usage encountered exists:

i) (relative) with **tam** meaning '**as... as...**':

> *quis tam formosus quam tu?*
> 'Who is *as* handsome *as* you?

ii) (relative) with **superlative adjectives or adverbs,** meaning '**as...as possible**':

---

[5] Learn these uses of the relative and interrogative pronouns as matters of vocabulary.

quam diligentissime studebat.
'He studied *as* hard *as possible*'.

iii) (relative) with **comparative adjectives or adverbs**, meaning '**than**'; Latin puts the two things being compared with each other in the same case:

nusquam urbs nobilior est quam Roma.
'Nowhere is there a city (nom.) more noble *than* Rome (nom.).'

iv) (relative) with **malo**, 'I prefer', and other phrases implying preference, comparison, etc., meaning '**than**':

nil aliud quam libros legere malo.
'I prefer nothing other *than* to read books.'

v) (relative) with **ante** or **post** (and other phrases denoting time, e.g. **postridie**), meaning respectively '**before**' or '**after**' etc.; *ante* and *post* are sometimes separated from *quam* by intervening words:

haec ante sunt gesta quam urbs condita est.
'These things were done *before* the city was founded.'

vi) (interrogative) **introducing questions**, both direct and indirect, in the sense of '**How...?**'

vos, iudices, scire volo quam necessarium hoc bellum sit.
'I want you to know, judges, *how* necessary this war is.'

vii) (exclamatory) **introducing exclamations**, in the sense of '**How...!**'

quam iuvat per florida prata ambulare!
'*How* pleasing it is to walk through flowery meadows!'

b) ***quod*** has three specific uses:
i) (relative) with both the indicative and the subjunctive, meaning '**because**' or '**inasmuch as**'; the **subjunctive** is used in place of the indicative in this sense to suggest that the reason given is **alleged** rather than substantiated:

> *Milo accusabatur quod Clodium necavisset.*
> 'Milo was accused *because (it was alleged)* he had killed Clodius.'

ii) (relative) with the indicative, meaning '**that**', '**the fact that**' or '**in that**'.

iii) (relative) preceding ***si***, ***nisi*** and conjunctions such as **cum** etc., meaning '**and**' or '**but**':

> *quod si illi ignosces, tibi gratiam reddet.*
> '*But* if you pardon (lit. will pardon) him, he will repay you the favour.'

c) The most common uses of ***quo*** are:
i) (interrogative) as an old dative form meaning '**to where/ which place?**' or, in a related sense, '**to what end/for what purpose?**':

> *quo ista facis?*
> '*To what end* are you doing those things of yours?'

ii) (interrogative) on its own or with ***loci*** or ***locorum***, meaning literally 'where of place(s)', hence '**where on earth?**'.

iii) (relative) in the phrase ***quo factum est***, meaning '**Therefore, it happened...** '.

iv) (relative) with the **subjunctive** and a **comparative adjective or adverb**, introducing a **purpose clause** (see **6. Purpose and Result Clauses Part 1 D**);

v) (relative) coupled with a **comparative adjective** or **adverb** and followed shortly by **eo** and a second comparative, meaning '**the more..., the more...**' etc.:

quo maior sumptus uxoris, eo pauperior vir.
'The *greater* the extravagance of the wife, the *poorer* the husband is.'

d) ***qua*** is used:
i) as an abbreviation of *qua via*, meaning '**by which route**', '**where**' or '**by which means**'.

ii) with a second ***qua***... to mean '**both...and...**', '**partly... partly...**':

... *qua cibi qua quietis immemor nox traducta est.* (Livy)
'...the night was spent heedless of *both* food *and* rest.'

e) ***qui*** occasionally occurs not as a nominative masculine singular or plural form, but as an old form of the ablative singular. This usage of ***qui*** most commonly introduces a question in the sense of '**how?**' or '**why?**'; in other contexts it means '**by which**' or '**with which**':

qui fit, Maecenas,...? (Horace)
'*How* does it happen, Maecenas,...?'

Exercises for Level Two[6]

Exercise 2A

The services of Pompey in securing Cicero's return from exile.

possum ego satis in Cn. Pompeium umquam gratus videri? **qui** non solum apud vos, **qui** omnes idem sentiebatis, sed etiam apud universum populum salutem[7] populi Romani et conservatam per me et coniunctam esse cum mea dixerit; **qui** causam meam prudentibus commendarit, imperitos edocuerit, eodemque tempore improbos auctoritate sua compresserit, bonos excitarit; **qui** populum Romanum pro me tamquam pro fratre aut pro parente non solum hortatus sit, verum etiam obsecrarit; **qui** cum[8] ipse propter metum dimicationis et sanguinis domo se teneret, iam a superioribus tribunis petierit ut[9] de salute mea et promulgarent et referrent;... **qui** cum[10] ipse mihi semper amicissimus fuisset, etiam ut[11] suos necessarios mihi amicos redderet elaborarit.

Cicero, *Oratio post Reditum in Senatu*

[6] All forms of *qui, quae, quod* etc., including those which belong to interrogative and indefinite pronouns, are highlighted in these exercises, in order to provide practice at distinguishing between these pronouns.

[7] *salutem...conservatam...et coniunctam esse*: see **2. Indirect Speech Part 2**.

[8] *cum...teneret*: see **4. Temporal Conjunctions E** vi).

[9] *ut...promulgarent et referrent*: see **2. Indirect Speech Part 5**.

[10] *cum...fuisset*: see **4. Temporal Conjunctions E** vi).

[11] *ut...redderet*: see **6. Purpose and Result Clauses Part 1 B** i).

Exercise 2B

Civilisation is of the highest importance.

sed **quo** sis, Africane, alacrior ad tutandam rem publicam[12], sic habeto[13]: omnibus, **qui** patriam conservaverint, adiuverint, auxerint, certum esse[14] in caelo ac definitum locum, ubi beati aevo sempiterno fruantur: nihil est enim illi principi deo, **qui** omnem hunc mundum regit, **quod** quidem in terris fiat, acceptius **quam** concilia coetusque hominum iure sociati, **quae** civitates appellantur; harum rectores et conservatores hinc profecti huc revertuntur.

Cicero, *Somnium Scipionis*

Exercise 2C

Epaminondas defends himself against the accusation of leaving no heirs.

hic uxorem numquam duxit. in **quo** cum[15] reprehenderetur, **quod** liberos non relinqueret, a Pelopida, **qui** filium habebat infamem, maleque eum in eo patriae consulere diceret, 'uide' inquit 'ne[16] tu peius consulas, **qui** talem ex te natum relicturus sis. neque uero stirps potest mihi deesse: namque ex me natam relinquo pugnam Leuctricam, **quae** non modo mihi superstes, sed etiam immortalis sit[17] necesse est.'

Cornelius Nepos

---

[12] *ad tutandam rem publicam*: see **5. Gerunds and Gerundives D** b) ii).
[13] *sic habeto*: 'know this'.
[14] *esse...locum*: see **2. Indirect Speech Part 2**.
[15] *cum reprehenderetur*: see **4. Temporal Conjunctions E** vi).
[16] *uide...ne*: 'See to it that...not'.
[17] *immortalis sit*: 'that it is...'.

Exercises for Level Three

Exercise 3A

Glorious examples of those who did not fear death.

sed quid ego Socratem aut Theramenem, praestantes viros virtutis et sapientiae gloria, commemoro? cum Lacedaemonius quidam, **cuius** ne nomen quidem proditum est, mortem tanto opere contempserit, ut, cum ad eam duceretur damnatus ab ephoris et esset vultu hilari atque laeto dixissetque ei quidam inimicus 'contemnisne leges Lycurgi?', responderit 'ego vero illi maximam gratiam habeo, **qui** me ea poena mulctaverit, **quam** sine mutuatione et sine versura possem dissolvere.' o virum Sparta dignum! ut mihi quidem, **qui** tam magno animo fuerit, innocens damnatus esse videatur. tales innumerabiles nostra civitas tulit. sed quid duces et principes nominem, cum legiones scribat Cato saepe alacres in eum locum profectas, unde redituras se non arbitrarentur? pari animo Lacedaemonii in Thermopylis occiderunt, in **quos** Simonides:

Dic, hospes, Spartae nos te hic vidisse iacentes,
dum sanctis patriae legibus obsequimur.

e **quibus** unus, cum Perses hostis in colloquio dixisset glorians 'solem prae iaculorum multitudine et sagittarum non videbitis', 'in umbra igitur', inquit, 'pugnabimus'. viros commemoro; qualis tandem Lacaena? **quae** cum filium in proelium misisset et interfectum audisset, 'idcirco', inquit, 'genueram, ut esset, **qui** pro patria mortem non dubitaret occumbere'.

Cicero, *Tusculan Disputations*

Exercise 3B

Tiberius' two marriages.

Agrippinam, Marco Agrippa genitam, neptem Caecili Attici equitis R., ad **quem** sunt Ciceronis epistulae, duxit[18] uxorem; sublatoque ex ea filio Druso, quanquam bene convenientem rursusque gravidam dimittere ac Iuliam Augusti filiam confestim coactus est ducere, non sine magno angore animi, cum et Agrippinae consuetudine teneretur et Iuliae mores improbaret, ut **quam** sensisset sui quoque sub priore marito appetentem, **quod** sane etiam vulgo existimabatur. sed Agrippinam et abegisse post divortium doluit et semel omnino ex occursu visam adeo contentis et umentibus oculis prosecutus est, ut custoditum sit ne umquam in conspectum ei posthac veniret. cum Iulia primo concorditer et amore mutuo vixit, mox dissedit et aliquanto gravius, ut etiam perpetuo secubaret, intercepto communis fili pignore, **qui** Aquileiae natus infans exstinctus est. Suetonius

Exercise 3C

Political servility.

exsequi sententias haud institui nisi insignes per honestum aut notabili dedecore, **quod** praecipuum munus annalium reor, ne uirtutes sileantur, utque prauis dictis factisque ex posteritate et infamia metus sit. ceterum tempora illa adeo infecta et adulatione sordida fuere, ut non modo primores ciuitatis, **quibus** claritudo sua obsequiis protegenda erat, sed omnes consulares, magna pars eorum **qui** praetura functi multique etiam pedarii senatores certatim exsurgerent foedaque et nimia censerent. memoriae proditur Tiberium, quotiens curia egrederetur, Graecis uerbis in hunc modum eloqui solitum 'o homines ad seruitutem paratos!' scilicet etiam illum, **qui** libertatem publicam nollet, tam proiectae seruientium patientiae taedebat. Tacitus, *Annals*

---

[18] *duxit*: the subject is Tiberius.

Exercises for Level Four

Exercise 4A

An occasional repulse makes the heart grow fonder.

si tibi non opus est seruata, stulte, puella,
　　at mihi fac serues, **quo** magis ipse uelim!
quod licet, ingratum est; **quod** non licet, acrius urit:
　　ferreus est, si quis, **quod** sinit alter, amat.
speremus pariter, pariter metuamus amantes,
　　et faciat uoto rara repulsa locum.
quo mihi fortunam, **quae** numquam fallere curet?
　　nil ego, **quod** nullo tempore laedat, amo!
uiderat hoc in me uitium uersuta Corinna,
　　quaque capi possem, callida norat opem.
a, quotiens sani capitis mentita dolores
　　cunctantem tardo iussit abire pede!
a, quotiens finxit culpam, quantumque licebat
　　insonti, speciem praebuit esse nocens!
sic ubi uexarat tepidosque refouerat ignis,
　　rursus erat uotis comis et apta meis.
quas mihi blanditias, **quam** dulcia uerba parabat,
　　oscula, di magni, qualia quotque dabat!

Ovid, *Amores*

Exercise 4B

Miltiades' advice is rejected.

eisdem temporibus Persarum rex Darius ex Asia in Europam exercitu traiecto Scythis bellum inferre decreuit. pontem fecit in Histro flumine, **qua** copias traduceret. eius pontis, dum ipse abesset, custodes reliquit principes, **quos** secum ex Ionia et Aeolide duxerat, **quibus** singulis ipsarum urbium perpetua dederat imperia. sic enim facillime putauit se Graeca lingua loquentes, **qui** Asiam incolerent, sub sua retenturum potestate, si amicis suis oppida tuenda tradidisset, **quibus** se oppresso nulla spes salutis relinqueretur. in hoc fuit tum numero Miltiades **cui** illa custodia crederetur. hic cum crebri afferrent nuntii male rem gerere Darium premique a Scythis, Miltiades hortatus est pontis custodes, ne a fortuna datam occasionem liberandae Graeciae dimitterent. nam si cum iis copiis, **quas** secum transportarat, interiisset Darius, non solum Europam fore tutam, sed etiam eos, **qui** Asiam incolerent Graeci genere, liberos a Persarum futuros dominatione et periculo: id facile effici posse. ponte enim rescisso regem uel hostium ferro uel inopia paucis diebus interiturum. ad hoc consilium cum plerique accederent, Histiaeus Milesius, ne res conficeretur, obstitit, dicens non idem ipsis, **qui** summas imperii tenerent, expedire et multitudini, **quod** Darii regno ipsorum niteretur dominatio: **quo** exstincto ipsos potestate expulsos ciuibus suis poenas daturos. itaque adeo se abhorrere a ceterorum consilio, ut nihil putet ipsis utilius **quam** confirmari regnum Persarum. huius cum sententiam plurimi essent secuti, Miltiades non dubitans tam multis consciis ad regis aures consilia sua peruentura, Chersonesum reliquit ac rursus Athenas demigrauit. **cuius** ratio etsi non ualuit, tamen magnopere est laudanda, cum amicior omnium libertati quam suae fuerit dominationi.

Cornelius Nepos

Exercise 4C

The achievements of great Romans through speaking.

quis enim putet aut celeritatem ingeni L. Bruto illi nobilitatis vestrae principi defuisse? **qui** de matre savianda ex oraculo Apollinis tam acute arguteque coniecerit; **qui** summam prudentiam simulatione stultitiae texerit; **qui** potentissimum regem clarissimi regis filium expulerit civitatemque perpetuo dominatu liberatam magistratibus annuis legibus iudiciisque devinxerit; **qui** conlegae suo imperium abrogaverit, ut e civitate regalis nominis memoriam tolleret: **quod** certe effici non potuisset, nisi esset oratione persuasum. videmus item paucis annis post reges exactos, cum plebes prope ripam Anionis ad tertium miliarium consedisset eumque montem, **qui** Sacer appellatus est, occupavisset, M. Valerium dictatorem dicendo sedavisse discordias eique ob eam rem honores amplissimos habitos et eum primum ob eam ipsam causam Maximum esse appellatum. ne L. Valerium quidem Potitum arbitror non aliquid potuisse dicendo, **qui** post decemviralem invidiam plebem in patres incitatam legibus et contionibus suis mitigaverit.

Cicero, *Brutus*

Exercises for Level Five

Exercise 5A

Hirtus apologises for finishing off Caesar's commentaries.

coactus assiduis tuis vocibus, Balbe, cum cotidiana mea recusatio non difficultatis excusationem sed inertiae videretur deprecationem habere, rem difficillimam suscepi. Caesaris nostri commentarios rerum gestarum Galliae, non comparantibus superioribus atque insequentibus eius scriptis, contexui, novissimumque imperfectum ab rebus gestis Alexandreae confeci usque ad exitum non quidem civilis dissensionis, cuius finem nullum videmus, sed vitae Caesaris. quos utinam qui legent scire possint quam invitus susceperim scribendos, quo facilius caream stultitiae atque arrogantiae crimine, qui me mediis interposuerim Caesaris scriptis. constat enim inter omnis nihil tam operose ab aliis esse perfectum quod non horum elegantia commentariorum superetur: qui sunt editi, ne scientia tantarum rerum scriptoribus desit, adeoque probantur omnium iudicio ut praerepta, non praebita facultas scriptoribus videatur. cuius tamen rei maior nostra quam reliquorum est admiratio: ceteri enim quam bene atque emendate, nos etiam quam facile atque celeriter eos perfecerit scimus. erat autem in Caesare cum facultas atque elegantia summa scribendi, tum verissima scientia suorum consiliorum explicandorum. mihi ne illud quidem accidit, ut Alexandrino atque Africano bello interessem; quae bella quamquam ex parte nobis Caesaris sermone sunt nota, tamen aliter audimus ea quae rerum novitate aut admiratione nos capiunt, aliter quae pro testimonio sumus dicturi. sed ego nimirum dum omnis excusationis causas colligo ne cum Caesare conferar, hoc ipso crimen arrogantiae subeo, quod me iudicio cuiusquam existimem posse cum Caesare comparari. vale. Hirtus

Exercise 5B

Attius Tullius contrives to have the Volscians expelled from Rome.

ludi quam amplissimi ut fierent senatus decreuit. ad eos ludos auctore Attio Tullio uis magna Volscorum uenit. priusquam committerentur ludi, Tullius, ut domi compositum cum Marcio fuerat, ad consules uenit; dicit esse quae secreto agere de re publica uelit. arbitris remotis, 'inuitus' inquit, 'quod sequius sit, de meis ciuibus loquor. non tamen admissum quicquam ab iis criminatum uenio, sed cautum ne admittant. nimio plus quam uelim, nostrorum ingenia sunt mobilia. multis id cladibus sensimus, quippe qui non nostro merito sed uestra patientia incolumes simus. magna hic nunc Volscorum multitudo est; ludi sunt; spectaculo intenta ciuitas erit. memini quid per eandem occasionem ab Sabinorum iuuentute in hac urbe commissum sit; horret animus, ne quid inconsulte ac temere fiat. haec nostra uestraque causa prius dicenda uobis, consules, ratus sum. quod ad me attinet, extemplo hinc domum abire in animo est, ne cuius facti dictiue contagione praesens uioler.' haec locutus abiit. consules cum ad patres rem dubiam sub auctore certo detulissent, auctor magis, ut fit, quam res ad praecauendum uel ex superuacuo mouit, factoque senatus consulto ut urbe excederent Volsci, praecones dimittuntur qui omnes eos proficisci ante noctem iuberent. ingens pauor primo discurrentes ad suas res tollendas in hospitia perculit; proficiscentibus deinde indignatio oborta, se ut consceleratos contaminatosque ab ludis, festis diebus, coetu quodam modo hominum deorumque abactos esse.

Livy

Exercise 5C

On the immortality of the soul.

non enim video, cur, quid ipse sentiam de morte, non audeam vobis dicere, quod eo cernere mihi melius videor, quo ab ea propius absum. ego vestros patres, P. Scipio tuque, C. Laeli, viros clarissimos mihique amicissimos, vivere arbitror et eam quidem vitam, quae est sola vita nominanda. nam dum sumus inclusi in his compagibus corporis, munere quodam necessitatis et gravi opere perfungimur; est enim animus caelestis ex altissimo domicilio depressus et quasi demersus in terram, locum divinae naturae aeternitatique contrarium. sed credo deos immortalis sparsisse animos in corpora humana, ut essent qui terras tuerentur quique caelestium ordinem contemplantes imitarentur eum vitae modo atque constantia. nec me solum ratio ac disputatio impulit ut ita crederem, sed nobilitas etiam summorum philosophorum et auctoritas. audiebam Pythagoran Pythagoriosque, incolas paene nostros, qui essent Italici philosophi quondam nominati, numquam dubitasse quin ex universa mente divina delibatos animos haberemus. demonstrabantur mihi praeterea quae Socrates supremo vitae die de immortalitate animorum disseruisset, is qui esset omnium sapientissimus oraculo Apollinis iudicatus. quid multa? sic mihi persuasi, sic sentio, cum tanta celeritas animorum sit, tanta memoria praeteritorum futurorumque prudentia, tot artes, tantae scientiae, tot inventa, non posse eam naturam, quae res eas contineat, esse mortalem; cumque semper agitetur animus nec principium motus habeat, quia se ipse moveat, ne finem quidem habiturum esse motus, quia numquam se ipse sit relicturus; et cum simplex animi natura esset neque haberet in se quicquam admixtum dispar sui atque dissimile, non posse eum dividi, quod si non posset, non posse interire; magnoque esse argumento homines scire pleraque ante quam nati sint, quod iam pueri, cum artis difficilis discant, ita celeriter res innumerabilis arripiant, ut eas non tum primum accipere videantur, sed reminisci et recordari. haec Platonis fere.

Cicero, *De Senectute*

Exercise 5D

A prophetic utterance spreads further terror.

terruerant satis haec pauidam praesagia plebem;
sed maiora premunt. nam qualis uertice Pindi
Edonis Ogygio decurrit plena Lyaeo,
talis et attonitam rapitur matrona per urbem
uocibus his prodens urguentem pectora Phoebum:
'quo feror, o Paean? qua me super aethera raptam
constituis terra? uideo Pangaea niuosis
cana iugis latosque Haemi sub rupe Philippos.
quis furor hic, o Phoebe, doce. quae tela manusque
Romanae miscent acies, bellumque sine hoste est?
quo diuersa feror? primos me ducis in ortus,
qua mare Lagaei mutatur gurgite Nili:
hunc ego, fluminea deformis truncus harena
qui iacet, agnosco. dubiam super aequora Syrtim
arentemque feror Libyen, quo tristis Erinys
transtulit Emathias acies. nunc desuper Alpis
nubiferae colles atque aeriam Pyrenen
abripimur. patriae sedes remeamus in urbis,
inpiaque in medio peraguntur bella senatu.
consurgunt partes iterum, totumque per orbem
rursus eo. noua da mihi cernere litora ponti
telluremque nouam; uidi iam, Phoebe, Philippos.'
haec ait, et lasso iacuit deserta furore.

Lucan, *De Bello Civili*

Chapter 11
COPING WITH *UT* AND *NE*

Parallel Revision: Vocabulary from Designated Vocabulary Exercises.

A. The purpose and arrangement of this chapter.

ut and *ne* have figured prominently in a number of previous chapters in a wide variety of functions. The primary purpose of this chapter is to provide a convenient overview of all these common functions by bringing them together in one place. In addition this chapter introduces a few further uses of *ut* and *ne*. The arrangement of the chapter reflects the manner in which *ut* and *ne* are encountered in texts, i.e. as different words, rather than as positive and negative methods of introducing the same individual constructions. Hence this chapter provides a synopsis of *ut* first, followed by a second separate synopsis of *ne*. These separate synopses may then be used as a tool to distinguish between the various functions of *ut* and *ne* as each is encountered in texts.

B. Coping with *ut*: the first steps

i) A common alternative form for *ut* is *uti*. Avoid confusing this with the visually identical present infinitive of *utor*.

ii) *ut* is found either with no verb at all or with an indicative or with a subjunctive. Since *ut* fulfils different functions in these different contexts and since these different functions lead to different translations, it is important to establish whether or not *ut* governs a verb and, if it does, to distinguish the **mood** of this verb, *before* attempting to translate.

iii) The contexts within which *ut* occurs are often characterised by features which help to identify the specific function of *ut*. These features include punctuation marks, words such as *tam* ('so...') or *eo* ('for this reason...') etc. Observation of such features usually provides the key to coping with *ut*. In the following, these features are highlighted in bold type, except in the table in section **E**, where they are listed in the first main column.

C. *ut* with no verb

When *ut* is found with **no verb**, it will normally mean '**as**':

te, ut mihi benevolentissimum, amo.
'I love you, *as* being most kind-hearted towards me.'

D. *ut* with the indicative

i) Where *ut* governs the **main verb** of a sentence and the sentence concludes with an **exclamation mark** or **question mark**, *ut* means '**How...!**' or '**How...?**' respectively:

ut multa variaque sunt hominum peccata!
'How many and varied are the transgressions of men!'

ii) Where an *indicative*-clause introduced by *ut* follows or precedes **a clause introduced by *sic* or *ita***, *ut* means '**as**':

ut ego haec filiis meis trado, sic hi suis tradent.
'Just as I am handing these things down to my sons, so they will hand them down to theirs.'

iii) Where neither of the above contexts exists, *ut* with an indicative most commonly means '**as**' or '**when**':

ut haec dixit, e curia egressus est.
'When he had said these things, he left the senate-house.'

E. *ut* with the subjunctive

The following table summarises the uses of *ut* described in previous chapters, with the final right hand column indicating the chapter and sub-section of the full description:

	Features to look for	**Type of Clause**	**Translate**	**Chapter**
i)	A preceding verb/(noun) of ordering, persuading or asking etc.	Indirect Command	'to…', 'that x should…'	**2. Part 5**
ii)	A preceding verb/(noun) expressing or implying questions	Indirect Question	'how…'	**2. Part 6**
iii)	A preceding *adeo, sic, tam, tantus, talis, tot* etc.	Result Clause	'that…'	**6. Part 2 A**
iv)	Sometimes a preceding *eo, ideo,* etc., but often no characteristic feature	Purpose Clause	'in order that…', 'in order to…' 'to…'	**6. Part 1 B** i)
v)	A preceding verb/(noun) expressing fear/anxiety	Negative Clause of Fearing	'that x might not'	**7. Part 1**
vi)	An independent subjunctive	Wish	'May…', 'If only…'	**8. D**

Here are three more usages of *ut* with the subjunctive:[1]

vii) *ut* with a subjunctive follows verbs meaning 'it happens (that)' or 'x brings it about (that)', e.g. ***accidit*** and ***evenit*** or ***efficio*** and ***perficio*** respectively. The subjunctive indicates no 'extra' or 'special' sense and should be translated without adding any 'should' or 'might' etc. Where a negative is required, *non* is used:

> *evenit ut quattuor horas pugnaretur.*
> 'It happened that they fought (lit. it was fought) for four hours.'
> *castris obsessis summa prudentia tamen imperator perfecit ut sui fame non conficerentur.*
> 'Although the camp was beseiged, with great wisdom however the commander brought it about that his men were not overcome by hunger.'

viii) *ut* occurs after impersonal verbs and verb-phrases, e.g. ***necesse est***, ***tantum abest***. Again the subjunctive should be translated without any 'should' etc.:

> *necesse est ut hostem cohibeant.*
> 'It is necessary that they hold back the enemy.'

ix) With a subjunctive *ut* occasionally means '**although**' or '**granted that**'; in this sense the *ut*-clause normally *precedes* the main clause:

> *ut huic proelio supersis, reliqua vita tibi dedecori erit.*
> '*Although* you may survive this battle, the rest of your life will bring you shame (lit. will be a source of shame to you).'

---

[1] *ut* may also precede *qui* + subjunctive to indicate a causal sense. See **10. Coping with *qui* D** iv).

F. *ne*

ne[2] occurs *only* with the **subjunctive** when used as a conjunction. The previous chapters discussed six uses of *ne*, as summarised in the following table:

	Features to look for	**Type of Clause**	**Translate**	**Chapter**
i)	A preceding verb/(noun) of ordering, persuading etc.	Indirect Command	'not to...', 'that x should not...'	**2. Part 5**
ii)	*Dum, dummodo* or *modo*	Proviso	'provided that...not'	**4. F** iv)
iii)	Sometimes a preceding *eo, ideo* etc., but often no characteristic feature	Purpose Clause	'in order that...not', 'not to...'	**6. Part 1 B** i)
iv)	A preceding verb/(noun) of fearing/anxiety	Positive Clause of Fearing	'that x might...'	**7. Part 1**
v)	An independent perfect subjunctive	Negative Direct Command	'Don't...!'	**8. B** ii)
vi)	An independent subjunctive, often with *utinam*	Wish or Exhortation	'May...not', 'If only... not', 'Let...not'	**8. D**

[2] *ne* is occasionally written in its older form *nei*.

To these six usages of *ne* may be added three more:

vii) *ne* occurs after verbs (or nouns) of **hindering**, **preventing** etc. in a manner similar to that of *quominus*.[3] As with *quominus*, translate '**from doing**':

nihil tibi obstat ne ad finem pervenias.
'Nothing is preventing you from reaching your goal.'

viii) *ne* occurs after verbs (or nouns) expressing caution, principally **caveo** and **vide/videte** in the sense 'take care'. Translate *ne* as '**lest**' or '**that...not**':

cave ne immoderate temereque facias.
'Take care that you do not act immoderately or rashly.'

ix) *ne* also occurs as an adverb in the phrase ***ne...quidem***, meaning '**not even**'. In this usage *ne* and *quidem* bracket the word or words to which they apply:

ne totus quidem exercitus eorum impetui resistere poterit.
'Not even the *entire* army will be able to resist their attack.'

[3] For *quominus*, see **7. Verbs of Fearing/*quominus* & *quin* Part 2 A** i).

Exercises for Level Two

Exercise 2A[V]

The following sentences contain clauses introduced by ut and ne in random order. Look for the features which help to identify the function of the clause and then translate.

a) tanta crudelitate res gerebat ut nemo ad eum accedere auderet.

b) saepe accidit ut homines se mala ambitione perdant.

c) Iason tauros flammiferos sub iugum egit, ut ei imperatum erat.

d) metuebam ne satis pecuniae egerem.

e) ut mihi amanti ianuae pateant!

f) ut Christiani in harenam producti patiuntur!

g) conspiratores nuntium miserunt ut rationem belli Manlio diceret.

h) timeo ut di hominum misereant.

i) servus fugitivus itineribus aviis progrediebatur ne custodibus incideret.

j) ut funem inciderant, nautae vela ventis intendebant.

Exercise 2B(i)

Pliny has collected and published his letters.

C. PLINIUS SEPTICIO CLARO SUO S.

frequenter hortatus es **ut** epistulas, si quas paulo curatius scripsissem,[4] colligerem publicaremque. collegi non servato temporis ordine (neque enim historiam componebam), sed **ut** quaeque in manus venerat. superest **ut** nec te consilii nec me paeniteat obsequii. ita enim fiet, **ut** eas quae adhuc neglectae iacent requiram et si quas addidero non supprimam. vale.

Pliny, *Letters*

Exercise 2B(ii)

Pliny asks Maximus to examine his book before publication.

C. PLINIUS MAXIMO SUO S.

et gaudium mihi et solacium in litteris, nihilque tam laetum quod his laetius, tam triste quod non per has minus triste. itaque et infirmitate uxoris et meorum periculo, quorundam vero etiam morte turbatus, ad unicum doloris levamentum studia confugi, quae praestant **ut** adversa magis intellegam sed patientius feram. est autem mihi moris, quod sum daturus in manus hominum, ante amicorum iudicio examinare, in primis tuo. proinde si quando, nunc intende libro quem cum hac epistula accipies, quia vereor **ne** ipse **ut** tristis parum intenderim. imperare enim dolori **ut** scriberem potui; **ut** vacuo animo laetoque, non potui. porro **ut** ex studiis gaudium sic studia hilaritate proveniunt. vale

Pliny, *Letters*

[4] *si...scripsissem*: see **9. Conditional Sentences C** iii).

Exercise 2C

Some men believe in gods, some do not.

sunt in fortunae qui[5] casibus omnia ponant
et nullo credant mundum[6] rectore moveri
natura volvente vices et lucis et anni,
atque ideo intrepidi quaecumque altaria tangunt.
est alius metuens **ne** crimen poena sequatur;
hic putat esse[7] deos et peierat, atque ita secum:
'decernat[8] quodcumque volet de corpore nostro
Isis et irato feriat mea lumina sistro,
dummodo[9] vel caecus teneam quos abnego nummos.
....
ut sit magna, tamen certe lenta ira deorum est;
si curant igitur cunctos punire nocentes,
quando ad me venient? sed et exorabile numen
fortasse experiar, solet his ignoscere. multi
committunt eadem diverso crimina fato:
ille crucem sceleris pretium tulit, hic diadema.'

Juvenal, *Satires*

---

[5] *qui...ponant...credant*: see **6. Purpose and Result Clauses Part 2 B**.
[6] *mundum...moveri*: see **2. Indirect Speech Part 2**.
[7] *esse deos*: see **2. Indirect Speech Part 2**.
[8] *decernat...feriat*: see **8. Independent Subjunctives B** i).
[9] *dummodo...teneam*: see **4. Temporal Conjunctions F** iv).

Exercises for Level Three

Exercise 3A

Delia is not to be trusted.

semper, **ut** inducar, blandos offers mihi uultus,
post tamen es misero tristis et asper, Amor.
quid tibi saeuitiae mecum est! an gloria magna est
insidias homini composuisse deum?
nam mihi tenduntur casses. iam Delia furtim
nescioquem tacita callida nocte fouet.
illa quidem tam multa negat, sed credere durum est;
sic etiam de me pernegat usque uiro.
ipse miser docui quo posset ludere pacto
custodes: eheu, nunc premor arte mea.
fingere tunc didicit causas **ut** sola cubaret,
cardine tunc tacito uertere posse fores.
tunc sucos herbasque dedi quis liuor abiret
quem facit impresso mutua dente Venus.
at tu, fallacis coniunx incaute puellae,
me quoque seruato peccet **ut** illa nihil.
neu iuuenes celebret multo sermone caueto,
neue cubet laxo pectus aperta sinu,
neu te decipiat nutu, digitoque liquorem
ne trahat et mensae ducat in orbe notas.
exibit cum saepe, time, seu uisere dicet
sacra Bonae maribus non adeunda Deae.
at mihi si credas, illam sequar unus ad aras;
tunc mihi non oculis sit timuisse meis.

Tibullus, *Elegies*

Exercise 3B

Caesar rushes to cross the Loire.

[Gallic forces gather near the banks of the Loire (*Liger*) in the hope of inspiring fear in the Romans and cutting them off from food supplies...]

quam ad spem multum eos adiuvabat quod Liger ex nivibus creverat, **ut** omnino vado non posse transiri videretur. quibus rebus cognitis Caesar maturandum sibi censuit, si esset in perficiendis pontibus periclitandum, **ut** prius quam essent maiores eo coactae copiae dimicaret. nam, **ut** commutato consilio iter in provinciam converteret, **ut ne** metu quidem necessario faciendum existimabat, cum infamia atque indignitas rei et oppositus mons Cevenna viarumque difficultas impediebat, tum maxime quod abiuncto Labieno atque eis legionibus quas una miserat vehementer timebat. itaque admodum magnis diurnis nocturnisque itineribus confectis contra omnium opinionem ad Ligerem venit, vadoque per equites invento pro rei necessitate opportuno, **ut** bracchia modo atque umeri ad sustinenda arma liberi ab aqua esse possent, disposito equitatu qui vim fluminis refringeret atque hostibus primo aspectu perturbatis incolumem exercitum traduxit; frumentumque in agris et pecoris copiam nactus, repleto his rebus exercitu iter in Senones facere instituit.

Caesar, *Bellum Gallicum*

Exercises for Level Four

Exercise 4A

Wounds of the heart resist healing.

hanc tibi Naso tuus mittit, Rufine, salutem:
qui miser est, ulli si suus esse potest.
reddita confusae nuper solacia menti
auxilium nostris spemque tulere malis.
ut que Machaoniis Poeantius artibus heros
lenito medicam vulnere sensit opem,
sic ego mente iacens et acerbo saucius ictu
admonitu coepi fortior esse tuo:
et iam deficiens sic ad tua verba revixi,
ut solet infuso vena redire mero.
non tamen exhibuit tantas facundia vires,
ut mea sint dictis pectora sana tuis.
ut multum demas nostrae de gurgite curae,
non minus exhausto quod superabit erit.
tempore ducetur longo fortasse cicatrix:
horrent admotas vulnera cruda manus.
non est in medico semper relevetur **ut** aeger:
interdum docta plus valet arte malum.
cernis **ut** e molli sanguis pulmone remissus
ad Stygias certo limite ducat aquas.
afferat ipse licet sacras Epidaurius herbas,
sanabit nulla vulnera cordis ope.

Ovid, *Epistulae ex Ponto*

Exercise 4B[10]

Decius Magius goes against the crowd.

ea **ne** fierent **neu** legatio mitteretur ad Poenum, summa ope Decius Magius, uir cui ad summam auctoritatem nihil praeter sanam ciuium mentem defuit, restiterat. **ut** uero praesidium mitti ab Hannibale audiuit, Pyrrhi superbam dominationem miserabilemque Tarentinorum seruitutem exempla referens, primo **ne** reciperetur praesidium palam uociferatus est, deinde **ut** receptum aut eiceretur aut, si malum facinus quod a uetustissimis sociis consanguineisque defecissent forti ac memorabili facinore purgare uellent, **ut** interfecto Punico praesidio restituerent Romanis se. haec – nec enim occulta agebantur – cum relata Hannibali essent, primo misit qui uocarent Magium ad sese in castra; deinde, cum is ferociter negasset se iturum nec enim Hannibali ius esse in ciuem Campanum, concitatus ira Poenus comprehendi hominem uinctumque attrahi ad sese iussit. ueritus deinde **ne** quid inter uim tumultus atque ex concitatione animorum inconsulti certaminis oreretur, ipse praemisso nuntio ad Marium Blossium, praetorem Campanum, postero die se Capuae futurum, proficiscitur e castris cum modico praesidio. Marius contione aduocata edicit, **ut** frequentes cum coniugibus ac liberis obuiam irent Hannibali. ab uniuersis id non obedienter modo sed enixe, fauore etiam uolgi et studio uisendi tot iam uictoriis clarum imperatorem, factum est. Decius Magius nec obuiam egressus est nec, quo timorem aliquem ex conscientia significare posset, priuatim se tenuit; in foro cum filio clientibusque paucis otiose inambulauit trepidante tota ciuitate ad excipiendum Poenum uisendumque. Hannibal ingressus urbem senatum extemplo postulat, precantibusque inde primoribus Campanorum **ne** quid eo die seriae rei

[10] The immediate background to this passage is provided by passage **1F** in Chapter 2.

gereret diemque **ut** ipse, aduentu suo festum, laetus ac libens celebraret, quamquam praeceps ingenio in iram erat, tamen, **ne** quid in principio negaret, uisenda urbe magnam partem diei consumpsit.

Livy

Exercise 4C

A teacher must be kept on his toes.

rara tamen merces quae cognitione tribuni
non egeat. sed vos saevas inponite leges,
ut praeceptori verborum regula constet,
ut legat historias, auctores noverit omnes
tamquam ungues digitosque suos, **ut** forte rogatus,
dum petit aut thermas aut Phoebi balnea, dicat
nutricem Anchisae, nomen patriamque novercae
Anchemoli, dicat quot Acestes vixerit annis,
quot Siculi Phrygibus vini donaverit urnas;
exigite **ut** mores teneros ceu pollice ducat,
ut si quis cera voltum facit; exigite **ut** sit
et pater ipsius coetus, **ne** turpia ludant,
ne faciant vicibus; non est leve tot puerorum
observare manus oculosque in fine trementis.
'haec', inquit, 'cura, sed cum se verterit annus,
accipe, victori populus quod postulat, aurum.'

Juvenal, *Satires*

Exercises for Level Five

Exercise 5A

M. Metilius argues that the dictator is not acting in the interests of the state.

de iis rebus persaepe et in senatu et in contione actum est. cum laeta ciuitate dictator unus nihil nec famae nec litteris crederet, ut uera omnia essent, secunda se magis quam aduersa timere diceret, tum M. Metilius tribunus plebis id unum enimuero ferendum esse negat, non praesentem solum dictatorem obstitisse rei bene gerendae sed absentem etiam gestae obstare ac sedulo tempus terere quo diutius in magistratu sit solusque et Romae et in exercitu imperium habeat. quippe consulum alterum in acie cecidisse, alterum specie classis Punicae persequendae procul ab Italia ablegatum; duos praetores Sicilia atque Sardinia occupatos, quarum neutra hoc tempore prouincia praetore egeat; M. Minucium magistrum equitum, ne hostem uideret, ne quid rei bellicae gereret, prope in custodia habitum. itaque hercule non Samnium modo, quo iam tamquam trans Hiberum agro Poenis concessum sit, sed et Campanum Calenumque et Falernum agrum peruastatos esse sedente Casilini dictatore et legionibus populi Romani agrum suum tutante. exercitum cupientem pugnare et magistrum equitum clausos prope intra uallum retentos; tamquam hostibus captiuis arma adempta. tandem, ut abscesserit inde dictator, ut obsidione liberatos, extra uallum egressos fudisse ac fugasse hostes. quas ob res, si antiquus animus plebei Romanae esset, audaciter se laturum fuisse de abrogando Q. Fabi imperio; nunc modicam rogationem promulgaturum de aequando magistri equitum et dictatoris iure. nec tamen ne ita quidem prius mittendum ad exercitum Q. Fabium quam consulem in locum C. Flamini suffecisset.

Livy

Exercise 5B

Pliny used a recitation as an opportunity to revise some light poetry.

C. PLINIUS ARRIANO SUO S.

ut in vita sic in studiis pulcherrimum et humanissimum existimo severitatem comitatemque miscere, ne illa in tristitiam, haec in petulantiam excedat. qua ratione ductus graviora opera lusibus iocisque distinguo. ad hos proferendos et tempus et locum opportunissimum elegi, utque iam nunc adsuescerent et ab otiosis et in triclinio audiri, Iulio mense, quo maxime lites interquiescunt, positis ante lectos cathedris amicos collocavi. forte accidit ut eodem die mane in advocationem subitam rogarer, quod mihi causam praeloquendi dedit. sum enim deprecatus, ne quis ut inreverentem operis argueret, quod recitaturus, quamquam et amicis et paucis, id est iterum amicis, foro et negotiis non abstinuissem. addidi hunc ordinem me et in scribendo sequi, ut necessitates voluptatibus, seria iucundis anteferrem, ac primum amicis tum mihi scriberem. liber fuit et opusculis varius et metris. ita solemus, qui ingenio parum fidimus, satietatis periculum fugere. recitavi biduo. hoc adsensus audientium exegit; et tamen ut alii transeunt quaedam imputantque quod transeant, sic ego nihil praetereo atque etiam non praeterire me dico. lego enim omnia ut omnia emendem, quod contingere non potest electa recitantibus. at illud modestius et fortasse reverentius; sed hoc simplicius et amantius. amat enim qui se sic amari putat, ut taedium non pertimescat; et alioqui quid praestant sodales, si conveniunt voluptatis suae causa? delicatus ac similis ignoto est, qui amici librum bonum mavult audire quam facere. non dubito cupere te pro cetera mei caritate quam maturissime legere hunc adhuc musteum librum. leges, sed retractatum, quae causa recitandi fuit; et tamen non nulla iam ex eo nosti. haec emendata postea vel, quod interdum longiore mora solet, deteriora facta quasi nova rursus et rescripta cognosces. nam plerisque mutatis ea quoque mutata videntur, quae manent. vale.

Pliny, *Letters*

Exercise 5C

Acontius insists that he will win over Cydippe.

pone metum! nihil hic iterum iurabis amanti;
    promissam satis est te semel esse mihi.
perlege! discedat sic corpore languor ab isto,
    quod meus est ulla parte dolere dolor!
quid pudor ante subit? nam, sicut in aede Dianae,
    suspicor ingenuas erubuisse genas.
coniugium pactamque fidem, non crimina posco;
    debitus ut coniunx, non ut adulter amo.
verba licet repetas, quae demptus ab arbore fetus
    pertulit ad castas me iaciente manus;
invenies illic, id te spondere, quod opto
    te potius, virgo, quam meminisse deam.
....
en, iterum scribo mittoque rogantia verba!
    altera fraus haec est, quodque queraris habes.
si noceo, quod amo, fateor, sine fine nocebo
    teque petam; caveas tu licet, usque petam.
per gladios alii placitas rapuere puellas;
    scripta mihi caute littera crimen erit?
di faciant, possim plures inponere nodos,
    ut tua sit nulla libera parte fides!
mille doli restant-clivo sudamus in imo;
    ardor inexpertum nil sinet esse meus.
sit dubium, possisne capi; captabere certe.
    exitus in dis est, sed capiere tamen.
ut partem effugias, non omnia retia falles,
    quae tibi, quam credis, plura tetendit Amor.
si non proficient artes, veniemus ad arma,
    inque tui cupido rapta ferere sinu.
non sum, qui soleam Paridis reprehendere factum,
    nec quemquam, qui vir, posset ut esse, fuit.
nos quoque-sed taceo! mors huius poena rapinae
    ut sit, erit, quam te non habuisse, minor.   Ovid, *Heroides*

Chapter 12

REVISION EXERCISES

Parallel Revision: All the grammar featured in *VIA PLANA*.

The passages included in this chapter have been chosen for their technical nature, i.e. each exhibits a concentration of different syntactical constructions. This variety of constructions renders the practice of highlighting specific syntactical constructions redundant. In its place advice is given for passages at the first two levels concerning which syntactical constructions it would be helpful to revise before translating. No such help is provided for levels three to five.

Exercise 1A

The points of grammar featured in these sentences occur in the same order as the chapters contained in this book.

a) Kalendis Martiis, qui dies 'Matronalia' vocatur, matronae Iunonem Martemque precantur servisque ipsis inter cenam serviunt.
b) fertur Romulum primum fuisse qui urbem muris saepserit.
c) laudi decorique est novo homini consul fieri.
d) cum primum eam conspicatus est, amore captus est.
e) rebus bene gerendis gloriam consequemur.
f) solusne est qui exta interpretari sciat?
g) Galli metu ne a Romanis opprimerentur subsidia admoverunt.
h) coronas tusque ad aras deorum afferamus!
i) nisi meam sententiam rogare metuisses, tibi verum dixissem.

Exercise 1B

The order of the topics featured in these sentences is random.

a) non dubito quin nobis semper laborandum sit.

b) cum Caesar ad castra advenerat, legiones eum imperatorem salutabant.

c) si ad virum adeas, eum mitem facilemque invenias.

d) vulnus ex adverso acceptum gloriae, a tergo dedecori militi est.

e) exploratores Caesarem monuere locum proelio haud aequum esse; copias ad clivum propinquum moveret, qui locus ad insidias aptior esset.

f) quid plura dicam? vobis memorem istius facinora scelestissima? minime, iudices: omnia enim iam scitis.

g) ne dimiseritis facultatem honores petendi.

h) ei qui beneficio maximo civitatem demeretur honor statuae redditur.

i) ne Minos quidem virginem illam amavit quae patrem patriamque proderet.

Exercise 1C(i): Revise Chs 1, 4-6.

Revision of books should be kept within reasonable limits.

C. PLINIUS ATRIO SUO S.

librum, quem misisti, recepi et gratias ago. sum tamen hoc tempore occupatissimus. ideo nondum eum legi, cum alioqui valdissime cupiam. sed eam reverentiam cum litteris ipsis tum scriptis tuis debeo, ut sumere illa nisi vacuo animo inreligiosum putem. diligentiam tuam in retractandis operibus valde probo. est tamen aliquis modus, primum quod nimia cura deterit magis quam emendat, deinde quod nos a recentioribus revocat simulque nec absolvit priora et incohare posteriora non patitur. vale.

Pliny, *Letters*

Exercise 1C(ii): Revise Chs 1-3, 7, 9

Pontius exceeded appropriate limits in his hospitality.

C. PLINIUS PONTIO SUO S.

scio quae tibi causa fuerit impedimento, quominus praecurrere adventum meum in Campaniam posses. sed, quamquam absens, totus huc migrasti: tantum mihi copiarum qua[1] urbanarum qua rusticarum nomine tuo oblatum est, quas omnes improbe, accepi tamen. nam me tui ut ita facerem rogabant, et verebar ne et mihi et illis irascereris, si non fecissem. in posterum nisi adhibueritis modum ego adhibebo; et iam tuis denuntiavi, si rursus tam multa attulissent, omnia relaturos. dices oportere me tuis rebus ut meis uti. etiam: sed perinde illis ac meis parco. vale.

Pliny, *Letters*

Exercise 1D(i)[2]: Revise Chs 1, 5-6, 9

Oh for the wings...

nunc ego Triptolemi cuperem consistere curru,
    misit in ignotam qui rude semen humum;
nunc ego Medeae vellem frenare dracones,
    quos habuit fugiens arce, Corinthe, tua;
nunc ego iactandas optarem sumere pennas,
    sive tuas, Perseu, Daedale, sive tuas:
ut tenera nostris cedente volatibus aura
    aspicerem patriae dulce repente solum,
desertaeque domus vultus, memoresque sodales,
    caraque praecipue coniugis ora meae.

Ovid, *Tristia*

---

[1] *qua...qua...*: 'both...and...'.

[2] Passage 1D(ii) follows on immediately from 1D(i). They have been separated here only for the sake of providing passages of suitable length.

Exercise 1D(ii): Revise Chs 1, 4-9

Ovid reminds himself that only Augustus has the power to grant his return.

stulte, quid haec frustra votis puerilibus optas,
quae non ulla tibi fertque feretque dies?
si semel optandum est, Augusti numen adora,
et, quem sensisti, rite precare deum.
ille tibi pennasque potest currusque volucres
tradere. det reditum, protinus ales eris.
si precer hoc (neque enim possum maiora rogare)
ne mea sint, timeo, vota modesta parum.
forsitan hoc olim, cum iam satiaverit iram,
tum quoque sollicita mente rogandus erit.

Ovid, *Tristia*

Exercise 1E: Revise Chs 1-2, 4-5, 8

Caesar hopes to achieve his goal without fighting.

Caesar in eam spem venerat se sine pugna et sine vulnere suorum rem conficere posse, quod re frumentaria adversarios interclusisset. cur etiam secundo proelio aliquos ex suis amitteret? cur vulnerari pateretur optime meritos de se milites? cur denique fortunam periclitaretur? praesertim cum non minus esset imperatoris consilio superare quam gladio. movebatur etiam misericordia civium, quos interficiendos videbat; quibus salvis atque incolumibus rem obtinere malebat.

Caesar, *Bellum Civile*

Now repeat the course at Level Two!

Exercises for Level Two

Exercise 2A: Revise Chs 1-4, 6-7, 9-10

Two letters of recommendation.

CICERO APPULEIO S.

L. Nostius Zoilus est coheres meus, heres autem patroni sui. ea re utrumque scripsi, ut et mihi cum illo causam amicitiae scires esse et hominem probum existimares, qui patroni iudicio ornatus esset. eum tibi igitur sic commendo ut unum ex nostra domo. valde mihi gratum erit, si curaris ut intellegat hanc commendationem sibi apud te magno adiumento fuisse.

CICERO REGI S.

A. Licinius Aristoteles Melitensis antiquissimus est hospes meus et praeterea coniunctus magno usu familiaritatis. haec cum ita sint, non dubito quin tibi satis commendatus sit; etenim ex multis cognosco meam commendationem plurimum apud te valere. hunc ego a Caesare liberavi; frequens enim fuerat nobiscum atque etiam diutius in causa est quam nos commoratus; quo melius te de eo existimaturum arbitror. fac igitur, mi Rex, ut intellegat has sibi litteras plurimum profuisse.

Cicero, *Letters*

Exercise 2B(i): Revise Chs 1-5, 11

A high tide causes panic.

eadem nocte accidit ut esset luna plena, qui dies maritimos aestus maximos in Oceano efficere consuevit, nostrisque id erat incognitum. ita uno tempore et longas navis, quibus Caesar exercitum transportandum curaverat quasque in aridum subduxerat, aestus compleverat et onerarias, quae ad ancoras erant deligatae, tempestas adflictabat, neque ulla nostris facultas aut administrandi aut auxiliandi dabatur. compluribus navibus fractis, reliquae cum essent funibus, ancoris, reliquisque armamentis amissis ad navigandum inutiles, magna, id quod necesse erat accidere, totius exercitus perturbatio facta est. neque enim naves erant aliae quibus reportari possent, et omnia deerant quae ad reficiendas navis erant usui et, quod omnibus constabat hiemare in Gallia oportere, frumentum his in locis in hiemem provisum non erat. Caesar, *Bellum Gallicum*

Exercise 2B(ii): Revise Chs 1-3, 5, 10-11

Caesar has the ships repaired.

L. Domitio App. Claudio consulibus, discedens ab hibernis Caesar in Italiam, ut quotannis facere consuerat, legatis imperat quos legionibus praefecerat uti quam plurimas possent hieme navis aedificandas veteresque reficiendas curarent. earum modum formamque demonstrat. ad celeritatem onerandi subductionesque paulo facit humiliores quam quibus in nostro mari uti consuevimus, atque id eo magis quod propter crebras commutationes aestuum minus magnos ibi fluctus fieri cognoverat; ad onera, ad multitudinem iumentorum transportandam paulo latiores quam quibus in reliquis utimur maribus. has omnis actuarias imperat fieri, quam ad rem multum humilitas adiuvat. ea quae sunt usui ad armandas navis ex Hispania apportari iubet. Caesar, *Bellum Gallicum*

Exercise 2C: Revise Chs 1, 4-5, 8-10

Nurture your relationship with your girlfriend carefully.

sed non, cui dederas a litore carbasa, uento
utendum, medio cum potiere freto.
dum nouus errat amor, uires sibi colligat usu;
si bene nutrieris, tempore firmus erit:
quem taurum metuis, uitulum mulcere solebas;
sub qua nunc recubas arbore, uirga fuit;
nascitur exiguus, sed opes adquirit eundo,
quaque uenit, multas accipit amnis aquas.
fac tibi consuescat: nil adsuetudine maius,
quam, tu, dum capias, taedia nulla fuge:
te semper uideat, tibi semper praebeat aures,
exhibeat uultus noxque diesque tuos.
cum tibi maior erit fiducia, posse requiri,
cum procul absenti cura futurus eris,
da requiem: requietus ager bene credita reddit,
terraque caelestes arida sorbet aquas...

Ovid, *Ars Amatoria*

Exercise 2D: Revise Chs 1-2, 4, 8-11

Make the most of your time.

tu ne quaesieris scire nefas, quem mihi, quem tibi
finem di dederint, Leuconoe, nec Babylonios
temptaris numeros. ut melius, quidquid erit, pati,
seu pluris hiemes seu tribuit Iuppiter ultimam,
quae nunc oppositis debilitat pumicibus mare
Tyrrhenum! sapias, vina liques, et spatio brevi
spem longam reseces. dum loquimur, fugerit invida
aetas: carpe diem, quam minimum credula postero.

Horace, *Odes*

Now the repeat the course at Level Three!

Exercises for Level Three

Exercise 3A

Scipio warns Jugurtha not to resort to bribery.

ea tempestate in exercitu nostro fuere conplures novi atque nobiles, quibus divitiae bono honestoque potiores erant, factiosi domi, potentes apud socios, clari magis quam honesti, qui Iugurthae non mediocrem animum pollicitando adcendebant, si Micipsa rex occidisset, fore uti solus imperi Numidiae potiretur: in ipso maxumam virtutem; Romae omnia venalia esse. sed postquam Numantia deleta P. Scipio dimittere auxilia et ipse revorti domum decrevit, donatum atque laudatum magnifice pro contione Iugurtham in praetorium abduxit ibique secreto monuit, ut potius publice quam privatim amicitiam populi Romani coleret neu quibus largiri insuesceret: periculose a paucis emi quod multorum esset. si permanere vellet in suis artibus, ultro illi et gloriam et regnum venturum: sin properantius pergeret, suamet ipsum pecunia praecipitem casurum. sic locutus cum litteris eum, quas Micipsae redderet, dimisit. earum sententia haec erat: 'Iugurthae tui in bello Numantino longe maxuma virtus fuit, quam rem tibi certo scio gaudio esse. nobis ob merita sua carus est; ut idem senatui et populo Romano sit, summa ope nitemur. tibi quidem pro nostra amicitia gratulor. habes virum dignum te atque avo suo Masinissa.'

Sallust, *Bellum Iugurthinum*

Exercise 3B

Martial's poetry is harmless.

spero me secutum in libellis meis tale temperamentum ut de illis queri non possit quisquis de se bene senserit, cum salua infimarum quoque personarum reuerentia ludant; quae adeo antiquis auctoribus defuit ut nominibus non tantum ueris abusi sint sed et magnis. mihi fama uilius constet et probetur in me nouissimum ingenium. absit a iocorum nostrorum simplicitate malignus interpres nec epigrammata mea scribat: inprobe facit qui in alieno libro ingeniosus est. lasciuam uerborum ueritatem, id est epigrammaton linguam, excusarem, si meum esset exemplum: sic scribit Catullus, sic Marsus, sic Pedo, sic Gaetulicus, sic quicumque perlegitur. si quis tamen tam ambitiose tristis est ut apud illum in nulla pagina Latine loqui fas sit, potest epistula uel potius titulo contentus esse. epigrammata illis scribuntur qui solent spectare Florales. non intret Cato theatrum meum aut, si intrauerit, spectet. uideor mihi meo iure facturus si epistulam uersibus clusero:

nosses iocosae dulce cum sacrum Florae
festosque lusus et licentiam uolgi,
cur in theatrum, Cato seuere, uenisti?
an ideo tantum ueneras, ut exires?

Martial

Exercise 3C

Tacitus summarises the history of the office of quaestor.

isdem consulibus P. Dolabella censuit spectaculum gladiatorum per omnes annos celebrandum pecunia eorum qui quaesturam adipiscerentur. apud maiores virtutis id praemium fuerat, cunctisque civium, si bonis artibus fiderent, licitum petere magistratus; ac ne aetas quidem distinguebatur, quin prima iuventa consulatum et dictaturas inirent. sed quaestores regibus etiam tum imperantibus instituti sunt, quod lex curiata ostendit ab L. Bruto repetita. mansitque consulibus potestas deligendi, donec eum quoque honorem populus mandaret. creatique primum Valerius Potitus et Aemilius Mamercus sexagesimo tertio anno post Tarquinios exactos, ut rem militarem comitarentur. dein gliscentibus negotiis duo additi, qui Romae curarent: mox duplicatus numerus, stipendiaria iam Italia et accedentibus provinciarum vectigalibus: post lege Sullae viginti creati supplendo senatui, cui iudicia tradiderat. et quamquam equites iudicia reciperavissent, quaestura tamen ex dignitate candidatorum aut facilitate tribuentium gratuito concedebatur, donec sententia Dolabellae velut venundaretur.

Tacitus, *Annals*

Exercise 3D

The poet asks his wife about the cause of her sadness.

quid mihi maesta die, sociis quid noctibus, uxor,
anxia pervigili ducis suspiria cura?
non metuo ne laesa fides aut pectore in isto
alter amor; nullis in te datur ire sagittis
-audiat infesto licet hoc Rhamnusia vultu-,
non datur. et si egomet patrio de litore raptus
quattuor emeritis per bella, per aequora lustris
errarem, tu mille procos intacta fugares,
non intersectas commenta retexere telas,
sed sine fraude palam, thalamosque armata negasses.
dic tamen, unde alta mihi fronte et nubila vultus?
anne quod Euboicos fessus remeare penates
auguror et patria senium componere terra?
cur hoc triste tibi? certe lascivia corde
nulla nec aut rapidi mulcent te proelia Circi
aut intrat sensus clamosi turba theatri;
sed probitas et opaca quies et sordida numquam
gaudia.

Statius, *Silvae*

Now repeat the course at Level Four!

Exercises for Level Four

Exercise 4A

The 'king'-bee offers a ruler a good example of clemency.

excogitare nemo quicquam poterit quod magis decorum regenti sit quam clementia, quocumque modo is et quocumque iure praepositus ceteris erit. eo scilicet formosius id esse magnificentiusque fatebimur, quo in maiore praestabitur potestate, quam non oportet noxiam esse si ad naturae legem componitur. natura enim commenta est regem, quod et ex aliis animalibus licet cognoscere et ex apibus; quarum regi amplissimum cubile est medioque ac tutissimo loco; praeterea opere vacat exactor alienorum operum, et amisso rege totum dilabitur, nec umquam plus unum patiuntur melioremque pugna quaerunt; praeterea insignis regi forma est dissimilisque ceteris cum magnitudine tum nitore. hoc tamen maxime distinguitur: iracundissimae ac pro corporis captu pugnacissimae sunt apes et aculeos in vulnere relinquunt, rex ipse sine aculeo est. noluit illum natura nec saevum esse nec ultionem magno constaturam petere telumque detraxit et iram eius inermem reliquit. exemplar hoc magnis regibus ingens; est enim illi mos exercere se in parvis et ingentium rerum documenta minima arguere. pudeat ab exiguis animalibus non trahere mores, cum tanto hominum moderatior esse animus debeat quanto vehementius nocet. utinam quidem eadem homini lex esset et ira cum telo suo frangeretur nec saepius liceret nocere quam semel nec alienis viribus exercere odia! facile enim lassaretur furor si per se sibi satis faceret et si mortis periculo vim suam effunderet.

Seneca, *De Clementia*

Exercise 4B

Dido wishes Aeneas to live.

non ego sum tanti-quid non censeris inique? -
ut pereas, dum me per freta longa fugis.
exerces pretiosa odia et constantia magno,
si, dum me careas, est tibi vile mori.
iam venti ponent, strataque aequaliter unda
caeruleis Triton per mare curret equis.
tu quoque cum ventis utinam mutabilis esses!
et, nisi duritia robora vincis, eris.
quid, si nescires, insana quid aequora possunt?
expertae totiens quam male credis aquae!
ut, pelago suadente etiam, retinacula solvas,
multa tamen latus tristia pontus habet.
nec violasse fidem temptantibus aequora prodest;
perfidiae poenas exigit ille locus,
praecipue cum laesus amor, quia mater Amorum
nuda Cytheriacis edita fertur aquis.
perdita ne perdam, timeo, noceamve nocenti,
neu bibat aequoreas naufragus hostis aquas.
vive, precor! sic te melius quam funere perdam.
tu potius leti causa ferere mei.

Ovid, *Heroides*

Exercise 4C

Caesar takes measures to protect the safety of individual soldiers whilst achieving his goal.

erat, ut supra demonstravimus, manus certa nulla, non oppidum, non praesidium quod se armis defenderet, sed in omnis partis dispersa multitudo. ubi cuique aut valles abdita aut locus silvestris aut palus impedita spem praesidi aut salutis aliquam offerebat, consederat. haec loca vicinitatibus erant nota, magnamque res diligentiam requirebat, non in summa exercitus tuenda (nullum enim poterat universis ab perterritis ac dispersis periculum accidere), sed in singulis militibus conservandis; quae tamen ex parte res ad salutem exercitus pertinebat. nam et praedae cupiditas multos longius evocabat et silvae incertis occultisque itineribus confertos adire prohibebant. si negotium confici stirpemque hominum sceleratorum interfici vellet, dimittendae plures manus diducendique erant milites; si continere ad signa manipulos vellet, ut instituta ratio et consuetudo exercitus Romani postulabat, locus ipse erat praesidio barbaris. neque ex occulto insidiandi et dispersos circumveniendi singulis deerat audacia. ut in eiusmodi difficultatibus, quantum diligentia provideri poterat providebatur, ut potius in nocendo aliquid praetermitteretur, etsi omnium animi ad ulciscendum ardebant, quam cum aliquo militum detrimento noceretur. dimittit ad finitimas civitates nuntios Caesar: omnis ad se vocat spe praedae ad diripiendos Eburones, ut potius in silvis Gallorum vita quam legionarius miles periclitetur, simul ut magna multitudine circumfusa pro tali facinore stirps ac nomen civitatis tollatur. magnus undique numerus celeriter convenit.

Caesar, *Bellum Gallicum*

Exercise 4D

Catullus requests a practical joke as a favour.

o Colonia, quae cupis ponte ludere longo,
et salire paratum habes, sed uereris inepta
crura ponticuli axulis stantis in rediuiuis,
ne supinus eat cauaque in palude recumbat:
sic tibi bonus ex tua pons libidine fiat,
in quo uel Salisubsali sacra suscipiantur,
munus hoc mihi maximi da, Colonia, risus.
quendam municipem meum de tuo uolo ponte
ire praecipitem in lutum per caputque pedesque,
uerum totius ut lacus putidaeque paludis
liuidissima maximeque est profunda uorago.
insulsissimus est homo, nec sapit pueri instar
bimuli tremula patris dormientis in ulna.
cui cum sit uiridissimo nupta flore puella
et puella tenellulo delicatior haedo,
adseruanda nigerrimis diligentius uuis,
ludere hanc sinit ut lubet, nec pili facit uni,
nec se subleuat ex sua parte, sed uelut alnus
in fossa Liguri iacet suppernata securi,
tantundem omnia sentiens quam si nulla sit usquam;
talis iste meus stupor nil uidet, nihil audit,
ipse qui sit, utrum sit an non sit, id quoque nescit.
nunc eum uolo de tuo ponte mittere pronum,
si pote stolidum repente excitare ueternum,
et supinum animum in graui derelinquere caeno,
ferream ut soleam tenaci in uoragine mula.

Catullus

Now repeat the course at Level Five!

Exercises for Level Five

Exercise 5A

Livy is glad to have recorded Rome's history from its beginnings.

facturusne operae pretium sim si a primordio urbis res populi Romani perscripserim nec satis scio nec, si sciam, dicere ausim, quippe qui cum ueterem tum uolgatam esse rem uideam, dum noui semper scriptores aut in rebus certius aliquid allaturos se aut scribendi arte rudem uetustatem superaturos credunt. utcumque erit, iuuabit tamen rerum gestarum memoriae principis terrarum populi pro uirili parte et ipsum consuluisse; et si in tanta scriptorum turba mea fama in obscuro sit, nobilitate ac magnitudine eorum me qui nomini officient meo consoler. res est praeterea et immensi operis, ut quae supra septingentesimum annum repetatur et quae ab exiguis profecta initiis eo creuerit ut iam magnitudine laboret sua; et legentium plerisque haud dubito quin primae origines proximaque originibus minus praebitura uoluptatis sint, festinantibus ad haec noua quibus iam pridem praeualentis populi uires se ipsae conficiunt: ego contra hoc quoque laboris praemium petam, ut me a conspectu malorum quae nostra tot per annos uidit aetas, tantisper certe dum prisca illa mente repeto, auertam, omnis expers curae quae scribentis animum, etsi non flectere a uero, sollicitum tamen efficere posset.

Livy

Exercise 5B

A long life is not always a blessing.

ut vigeant sensus animi, ducenda tamen sunt
funera natorum, rogus aspiciendus amatae
coniugis et fratris plenaeque sororibus urnae.
haec data poena diu viventibus, ut renovata
semper clade domus multis in luctibus inque
perpetuo maerore et nigra veste senescant.
rex Pylius, magno si quicquam credis Homero,
exemplum vitae fuit a cornice secundae.
felix nimirum, qui tot per saecula mortem
distulit atque suos iam dextra conputat annos,
quique novum totiens mustum bibit. oro, parumper
attendas quantum de legibus ipse queratur
fatorum et nimio de stamine, cum videt acris
Antilochi barbam ardentem, cum quaerit ab omni
quisquis adest socius, cur haec in tempora duret,
quod facinus dignum tam longo admiserit aevo.
haec eadem Peleus, raptum cum luget Achillem,
atque alius cui fas Ithacum lugere natantem.
incolumi Troia Priamus venisset ad umbras
Assaraci magnis sollemnibus Hectore funus
portante ac reliquis fratrum cervicibus inter
Iliadum lacrimas, ut primos edere planctus
Cassandra inciperet scissaque Polyxena palla,
si foret extinctus diverso tempore, quo non
coeperat audaces Paris aedificare carinas.
longa dies igitur quid contulit? omnia vidit
eversa et flammis Asiam ferroque cadentem.
tunc miles tremulus posita tulit arma tiara
et ruit ante aram summi Iovis ut vetulus bos,
qui domini cultris tenue et miserabile collum
praebet ab ingrato iam fastiditus aratro.

Juvenal, *Satires*

Exercise 5C

The people above all must judge who is the best orator.

etenim necesse est, qui ita dicat, ut a multitudine probetur, eundem doctis probari. nam quid in dicendo rectum sit aut pravum ego iudicabo, si modo is sum qui id possim aut sciam iudicare; qualis vero sit orator ex eo quod is dicendo efficiet poterit intellegi. tria sunt enim, ut quidem ego sentio, quae sint efficienda dicendo: ut doceatur is apud quem dicetur, ut delectetur, ut moveatur vehementius. quibus virtutibus oratoris horum quidque efficiatur aut quibus vitiis orator aut non adsequatur haec aut etiam in his labatur et cadat, artifex aliquis iudicabit. efficiatur autem ab oratore necne, ut ei qui audiunt ita afficiantur ut orator velit, vulgi adsensu et populari adprobatione iudicari solet. itaque numquam de bono oratore aut non bono doctis hominibus cum populo dissensio fuit. an censes, dum illi viguerunt quos ante dixi, non eosdem gradus oratorum vulgi iudicio et doctorum fuisse? de populo si quem ita rogavisses: quis est in hac civitate eloquentissimus? in Antonio et Crasso aut dubitaret aut hunc alius, illum alius diceret. nemone Philippum tam suavem oratorem, tam gravem, tam facetum his anteferret, quem nosmet ipsi, qui haec arte aliqua volumus expendere, proximum illis fuisse diximus? nemo profecto; id enim ipsum est summi oratoris summum oratorem populo videri.

Cicero, *Brutus*

Exercise 5D

On sleep.

nunc quibus ille modis somnus per membra quietem
irriget atque animi curas e pectore solvat,
suavidicis potius quam multis versibus edam;
parvus ut est cycni melior canor, ille gruum quam
clamor in aetheriis dispersus nubibus austri.
tu mihi da tenuis auris animumque sagacem,
ne fieri negites quae dicam posse retroque
vera repulsanti discedas pectore dicta,
tutemet in culpa cum sis neque cernere possis.
principio somnus fit ubi est distracta per artus
vis animae partimque foras eiecta recessit
et partim contrusa magis concessit in altum.
dissoluuntur enim tum demum membra fluuntque.
nam dubium non est, animai quin opera sit
sensus hic in nobis, quem cum sopor impedit esse,
tum nobis animam perturbatam esse putandumst
eiectamque foras; non omnem; namque iaceret
aeterno corpus perfusum frigore leti.
quippe ubi nulla latens animai pars remaneret
in membris, cinere ut multa latet obrutus ignis,
unde reconflari sensus per membra repente
posset, ut ex igni caeco consurgere flamma?

Lucretius, *De Rerum Natura*